HOW TO BECOME THE TRUE *You*

Onereon through Jeff Michaels

Other Books by Jeff Michaels

Harmonic Coalescence

Touch the Earth: A Path to Ascension

Beings: A Journey to Joy

Light: The Reason for Existence

HOW TO BECOME THE TRUE *You*

Onereon through Jeff Michaels

LIGHT Technology PUBLISHING

For more information about special discounts for bulk purchases, please contact Light Technology Publishing Special Sales at 1-800-450-0985 (U.S. Only), 928-526-1345, or publishing@LightTechnology.net.

Also available as an e-book from your favorite e-book distributor.

ISBN-13: 978-1-62233-032-4
Published and printed in the United States of America by:

Light Technology Publishing

PO Box 3540
Flagstaff, AZ 86003
1-800-450-0985 • 928-526-1345
www.LightTechnology.com

Contents

Dedication

To Jill, without whom I would not be the being I am today, and to all of the beings who exist in and around this planet, especially those who help us ask, "Who am I?"

Regarding You

There is a deceptive simplicity to the question, "Who are you?" When we are asked it, we often respond with our names or perhaps our occupations. Sometimes we refer to our families. We are always implying that we exist within a greater community, and we validate ourselves by speaking of the connections we have been born into or have formed. These answers, once accepted, serve to deepen our belief that the statements are indicators of our identities.

However, when the question is turned about and asked internally, it becomes, "Who am I?" The same answers we give to someone asking, "Who are you?" often seem pale and weak in our personal quests. We seek deeper meaning. A simple recitation of where we live or who our parents are does little to bring a sense of satisfaction to our inner selves.

Not everyone is able or willing to ask, "Who am I?" It can be the start of life-changing action. When we begin this quest, we are inviting meaningful life change. Only when we take ourselves out of the context of our families, our communities, or our tribes can we begin to test our strengths and expose our weaknesses. Not everyone possesses the type of courage necessary to begin such a journey. And once begun, that journey requires courage and persistence as well.

The only place one finds the answer is within. No amount of external validation will support the seeker in finding the pure, clear truth of who he or she actually is. As time passes, we shift, alter, grow, and adapt. The knowledge that serves us as children must fade when confronted by new perceptions and events. The acceptance of boundaries and rules in youth must transform as we learn new responses to life and gain access to new abilities that assist us in dealing with an ever-changing world.

The world today is vastly different from the one of the recent past. The promise of even greater change is ever present. Only the one who consistently seeks new paths of response and increases personal abilities will be able to weather the coming shift of energies on planet Earth.

We all face amazing changes as we enter an age when the evolution of human society becomes swifter and reaches further than any time in history. The answers to such deep questions as "Who am I?" or "What is the meaning of life?" are fluid, and they require the seeker to be uncompromising in self-perception. Asking them creates a need for truth and transparency, and it begins within each person.

No one can answer the questions posed except the individual: You. The understanding that the answer today will be different from the answer tomorrow will set you apart from most people.

Perhaps it would be good to ask the question in a slightly different way: "Who am I truly?"

You cannot be the you of the past.

You are not yet the you of the future.

You are who you are today. And the truth is tomorrow you will change. Are you willing to ask the question and create the change? Or would you rather let the questions fade from your consciousness so that you merely exist?

Who is the true you?

— Jeff Michaels

An Introduction to the Onereon Channelings

Onereon (pronounced "O nair ee on") is a group of beings who define themselves as "together." They indicate that, during channeling, anyone who is in the room is a potential member of Onereon, for we are together. This will also hold true for those who read these pages. The group describes this togetherness not necessarily as an agreement but as a direction of energy, as togetherness in purpose.

The beings of Onereon currently come through to me in three main personalities, each distinct with a definite point of view. I often describe them as a human resources department, as if we are all working for a cosmic company. There are others in this human resources department, but they do not come through as often.

A great deal of humor and compassion comes through during the channeling sessions. When reading the transcriptions, be aware of the wryness and the sometimes-ironic tone that the communications contain. There is always underlying warmth in the comments as well, which I find comforting and invigorating.

Above all else, the Onereon group believes in us and in our ability to grow and evolve. Much of what the beings say is indicative of the future of humanity and the vitality of the planetary system that we are a part of, Gaia and her companion.

They point out that we are not as important physically as we are as energetic beings who have existed essentially forever; we are, in fact, aspects of Source, the singular energy of creation. Whatever form we take is an equally important expression of creation. They also point out that we are not the pinnacle of creation. For some people, this information may seem disappointing.

However, the Onereon beings also point out that they are not the pinnacle of creation either. They are quick to include themselves in the "not as important" category. The phrase used to open the channeling sessions, "As above, so below," applies equally to those in the spirit realm as it does to us in the physical realm.

Frequent references to the idea of body, mind, and spirit punctuate the channelings, helping us to understand the need to stay grounded in the physical world while we pursue our spiritual pathways and goals. Of the word "mind" used in the phrase "body, mind, and spirit," Onereon is quick to indicate that it does not simply refer to the way we think or how we use our intellectual capacities; it also implies the balance of emotional energies of the heart with the logic energies of the brain. Therefore, the term "mind" takes on the meaning of the heart and the brain working together. Spirit, the beings say, cannot be comprehended by logic but only by emotion. Still, spirit is ultimately logical.

Onereon also speaks of us as energetic beings in the same way that we can describe water. Once we change, such as in birth or death, we are not the same personalities. We recombine and become different from what we were in the same way as a drop of water goes into a pool and joins its molecules with other water molecules. The chances, then, of the individual molecules coming together to form the exact same drop as it once had been are extremely slim. In this same way, we do not come back to Earth as the same personality or even the same species as we once were! Yet we remain life energy, sometimes in physical form and sometimes in spirit form. The reasons for this are explained through the channelings.

A change is coming in the way that we will communicate. Onereon indicates that this change has been going on for about 200 years and will continue another 100 or so. The group points out that our way of communicating has already changed and continues to change dramatically in the physical realm. "So below," the beings say, then also "as above." In other words, look at how fast we communicate with each other on the planet now, and you will have a clue about how fast we will communicate with those in the spirit realm in the future.

Onereon reminds us that we, as human beings, have reached a level of maturity at which we must take responsibility for our lives and our future. The time for continually calling on spirit as guides or angels to grant us some favor or blessing will soon pass. We are capable of doing many of these things ourselves and of creating what we choose for our lives on the planet. The beings encourage us to see those in the spirit realm more as companions, fellow spiritual seekers, and partners in the enjoyment of all creation on all levels.

Onereon indicates that we are returning to a way of life in which spirit and body are not separated but are joined and have a balanced mind that acts in concert with and grows toward a peaceful future, not just for life on Earth but throughout the universe in all its forms. I am happy to have been chosen as the voice of this warm, wise, and witty group and am pleased to be able to present to you this information as I am allowed to perceive it.

Entries may have been edited for better understanding in the written form, otherwise the content remains uniquely Onereon's own.

CHAPTER ONE

Your Family of Guides

As above, so below. We are Onereon. We are a group of spiritual beings dedicated to ensuring that all beings on the planet receive the opportunity to enjoy life to the fullest and expand their karmic paths. We are a specific family and possess this specific purpose. Perhaps you are a member of this family. Perhaps your purpose is more closely associated with another group. We now seek to help you improve your communication with those of your spiritual family.

There are many family groups on the planet today. Through DNA, you are related to all beings. Beyond Earth there are also families and groups of beings to which you are related. Understand that there is a higher level to DNA, a sort of energetic genetics. At this level of existence, there are many purposes, and our paths are more specific than are made clear when we are alive upon the planet. You may already be aware that you possess a close vibration with some spiritual beings. In this, you may wish for a clearer communication as to your purpose or path while you are incarnate on Earth.

For many, it is difficult to receive communication from the realm of spirit. There is much in the world that interrupts the flow of communication. How can you maintain your connection in these very psychically noisy times? The responsibility is not solely yours, but you can increase the connection through particular practices.

First, understand that when you receive guidance, it is often nothing more than a higher perspective. What might look like an insurmountable problem to you is, in reality, a simple obstacle. Stepping back from a problem can give you a better perspective from which to examine it. Your spiritual guides can frequently point you to an easier path, but you must take the steps.

Second, understand that each one of us, every being at every vibrational level, serves a specific purpose in the course of events. This is not the same as preordination or destiny. A purpose carries with it the opportunity for variation and innovation. Discovery of purpose is a necessary step toward raising your vibration. It is not so hard to learn. Questions directed to your spiritual family group can be phrased in such a way as to gain insight on their higher purpose. While on the planet, you might think your purpose may be more detailed and seem less grand. It is still important. Accomplishment of one level of your purpose will lead to another, higher level, often with more responsibility attached to it. It is this realization of responsibility that slows many people down. Do not fear to grow in your ability to respond to all creation.

Third, release the thought that your spiritual family needs some form of worship or sacrifice. We in the spirit realm are much like you incarnate on the planet. There are differences, but we all stem from the same source of energy. We all have the ability to gain access to that source. We are not more important than you. The simple truth is that, at times, you are here in the realm of spirit while many of us return to the planet. In this way, you have been our guides in the past and will be again in the future! This should shape your vision of yourself. In a way, this thought will make life more serious. It also creates more freedom for you. With greater freedom comes greater responsibility. We offer you direction. We do not offer commandments. Your choices are the important thing.

A Two-Way Path

Communication is two directional. You should not always wait for your spiritual guides to initiate the relationship. You must commune with your spiritual family and get to know them. The best and easiest way to accomplish a close relationship is by sharing personal experiences. Invite them to observe things through your senses, such as the feel of cool water or the sight of beautiful scenery. This can not only bring you closer to them but also heighten your own appreciation of life in the physical realm. Offer to share with them physical experiences, and you will receive in return shared spiritual sensations.

Many members of the family human expect a conversation in which one being asks a question and the other responds. The nature of the spiritual realm is not one of physical senses as you comprehend them. It is more in the manner of groupings of thought or emotion. You can ask a question through either thought or voice, but a direct verbal answer is not likely. You must learn to trust the inner voice. It is often your own intuition, but this is exactly where the messages from beyond the physical realm enter your consciousness. Your brain can and often does translate the communication into words. It is true with this very channeling. The thoughts came in a group to the channel, and he then translated and made it a more linear communication.

Even in this method of communicating, there is a higher wisdom. Free will is inherent in you. This is a spiritual quality. You decide how best to use the information offered. There is rarely a straight dictum or ruling offered in true guidance. Advice is given. It is yours to interpret and act on. In the asking, there is also wisdom.

The Subject of Angels

Much is misunderstood about those called angels. There is no specific class or family that carries the name exclusively. The meaning and action of a being identified as an angel is that of bringing a message. This is beyond simple communication. These messages carry a higher vibration and are often of great importance to the recipients.

In some cases, the message can take the form of a warning. You may experience a forceful feeling not to pursue a certain course or enter a specific situation. This can sometimes be so acute as to affect you physically. It may be that others can easily take part in the same situation without adverse effects. It may be that the message is specifically for you.

Alternately, there can be a feeling of great joy or happiness. This is a pronouncement of beneficial changes to you or even the entirety of the family human. A message such as this almost always carries with it a deeper spiritual sense and meaning. There have been far more of these types of angelic communications coming from the spirit realm than warnings. In fact, most often the source of warnings is deep within you. Remember that you are powerfully connected with spiritual life, so you can and should regularly tap into the same flow of energy that we in the spirit realm do. This leads to clear guidance that comes from your own spiritual nature.

Note that angelic activity is not limited to spirit beings. Many members of the family human are acting in such a way today. Not only humanity but also members of the animal realm serve in the capacity of delivering angelic messages. Each year, more are being added to the ranks of those who can be called angelic. Soon many messages will be received by many across the planet. These will be calls to action in many cases. They will be sent with individual recipients in mind. The instructions will be tailored for the specific being.

An angelic message is not one that carries fear, division, or anger. You will know a true angelic spiritual message by the use of particular terms: the encouragement to change; the exhortation to question existing traditions, laws, philosophies, or beliefs; the call to greater responsibility regarding the health of all beings; and the direction to let all beings enjoy life and loving relationships. These are words that indicate a higher vibrational state. Acting in accord with these messages and with those who deliver them will not simply raise your own vibration but will increase the space for higher levels of spiritual life in the physical realm. The communication with your guides will shift easily to one of companionship and friendship.

The spiritual cooperation that you long for is near. We too desire this reality. It is the product of tens of thousands of years of growth through much difficulty and strife. We in the spirit realm have done our best to clear the path between the physical and spiritual realms. We are all closer now than we have been in many, many lifetimes. It is time for those alive in the physical realm to clarify their thoughts and emotions.

Focus on the qualities we communicate to you. You know them and recognize these aspects from all of your spiritual traditions. They are qualities integral to your very essence, your deepest core. We speak them now: Joy to you and all those in your circle. Peace to all who enter into life on the planet. Love to everyone and everything in existence. These communications conquer all challenges.

CHAPTER TWO

Who Is the True You?

As above, so below. In the near future, important questions will arise for those on the planet and those in a slightly higher realm. Your answers will assist in determining the course of the next generations. We have often said that you are beings who possess the ability to manifest for yourselves. Many of you do this on a personal level daily. What you and the coming generations are being asked to do is manifest on a global scale. This may seem daunting. It may feel impossible, but we assure you that the task is being approached and supported in ways that you cannot yet comprehend. You are not alone!

What Is the Most Vital Question?

Who are you at your core? Who are you at the deepest level of your karmic entity? Who would you be if there were no other influences pressing against you? What would you think and feel? What would your strongest desires be?

These questions are not only difficult and thought provoking but also tricky. They are difficult because you have already been influenced by your experiences on the planet. You are already formed and shaped in ways that have redirected your original karmic energies. To answer these questions, you must be willing to release all the notions you may have not just about who you are but also about what you believe. True spiritual seekers will have no fear in this regard. They will not be attached to a belief system and will be open to a course correction. There are those who will seek to defend the positions they hold. These are not the people who will cocreate the future. How can they be when they are entrenched in the past?

To ask yourself, "What is my true karmic purpose?" is to begin a process of release that will change what is important to you on the planet. Do not ask the question lightly. Once it is spoken, the process begins. You will instantly feel larger, and it will not be easy to return to the small place where you now exist.

Where Are You?

The being that is you on this planet is attached to a much larger energy. In truth, there is no real separation of the energies of the universe; there are only variations in vibration. What is perceived as a boundary is merely a moment when vibrations phase differently. All things are vibrations. There are no true boundaries. Imagine a rainbow and think of the spectrum of colors as one fades into another. Imagine a singer raising the notes on a scale with no pause from one to the next. It is this way with all things. What appears to be a boundary is simply the observer's limited perception. It is this way with your physical life as time moves you in a specific direction. There is no boundary or line that you cross as you age. It is a smooth process. Only when you place artificial lines on your physical life do you begin to feel constricted and held to certain pressures.

The choices that you make indicate who you are. Do you act from the energy of love? If you say yes, then you must be someone who releases the need to judge others' choices. You would be a being who needs no exterior validation of or insignia for your belief system. Your actions would radiate the energy of love. This is a difficult path to follow in today's world.

The activities a being enjoys can reveal the level of its vibration. Consider how humans react to their experiences. Some enjoy music that others feel disturbed by. Those who revel in violence, confrontation, or extremely loud rhythm may not be capable of perceiving higher vibrational opportunities at this moment. This is not a judgment of or a call to judge them. Little can be labeled as wrong in the universal energies, but much can be identified as unbalanced.

What Is Being Filtered?

Because you are a being seeking higher spiritual levels of existence, your choices are important. We have said that the planet is a filter. Each incarnation you experience is a part of that filtering, and each choice you make in life is a part of that process. What exactly is being filtered? Some may think that it is negative energy. We tell you now that there is no such thing as positive or negative energy; there is only energy. You may perceive a certain action of energy as negative because of the way you react to or are directly affected by it. The truth is greater than your personal response to events.

This is not said to make you feel small or unworthy. The opposite is true. It is said so that you may raise your perception and, in doing so, create a space for a higher vibrational action to occur. What is being filtered is the imbalance of the energies of Source. The equalization of Source energy will eventually bring everything into a balanced existence without losing the diversity that now exists. The diversity will be a continuum of harmony. This is important for spiritually minded beings to remember. The universe does not support conformity; it does support diversity. Any effort or movement made to create a uniform society is contrary to the very nature of existence.

It is also important to realize that the universe does not support violence or confrontation. All the physical laws that govern things of all sizes, from galaxies to subatomic structures, work to help things combine and balance. Some destruction is observable, but this is all part of the process of Source seeking balance. Be cautious not to label occurrences as destructive when they can more easily be described as transformative. This is releasing judgment, which is a vital component to the filtering process on the planet.

Releasing judgment in your life, in your present incarnation, will allow a power to flow through you that filters other imbalances. You will, of course, have to face the situations and deal with the things and beings that are in a state of imbalance. The first of these is yourself!

Who Are You at Your Karmic Core?

We said earlier that you have assistance, that you are not alone in this work. We said that the work is not truly difficult and that many are involved making the activity lighter. By taking on this task and answering these questions, you set a pattern for the next generation and the one after that. We will speak more regarding the children at a later time. For now, you are the focus.

The coming years are crucial. You are reaching a crossroad for the planet. What has been in preparation for several decades begins in earnest now. Some of you are new to this particular work, and some of you are longtime seekers of spiritual knowledge. All of you are vital, and we in the realm of spirit now ask for you to take a stronger spiritual stance. What this means is to act daily in ways that reflect deep spiritual principles, behave as if you are already in spirit and are responding to requests made by those you encounter on the planet, and conduct yourself in a way that has been termed angelic or as a messenger of spirit.

In times of choice, choose the path of love. In times of decision, decide on the course that opens the future for growth. Do not look back. Accept the newer ideas and move ahead, even if you are uncertain how things will actually work or function. The true spiritual being has the ability to manifest what is needed at any given moment.

In these moments, you create the future. In these moments, you bridge the past and the future. You have stood between one reality and another. You have been given the first true visions of the future. It is by your actions now that others accept these new realities before they arrive. Step away from the past and look to yourself as a larger, higher-vibrational karmic entity. In taking these steps, you release the pressures that prevent peace and joy from existing around you.

The source of all things is love. When you find you are in a state of imbalance, seek to return to your original energy from before you were born. Regain that perception of love, and observe how obstacles and problems fade in the light of love.

Who are you at your karmic core? You cannot be anything but love.

CHAPTER THREE

Who Are You Now?

As above, so below. We ask, "Who are you now?" so that you may begin to gain a clearer perspective regarding what you have all gone through in the past decades. We will use linear terminology to be clear, but we encourage you to remain loose in your attachment to concepts like straight lines, calendar demarcations, and clocks. Many of you are already stepping away from timelines and preconceived notions of aging.

What Just Happened?

What has happened to the galaxy is a natural thing but not a common occurrence. There are rhythms to the entire universe. Wave actions take place in many ways. The lack of creative and growth energy on the planet in recent decades can be compared to a low, low tide at the shore of an ocean. What happens after a low tide? A rising tide, of course. This is where you are in the stream of time: Energetic availability is increasing for everyone on the planet. Indeed, this entire section of the galaxy will see more activity and kinetic movement.

This increase in energy comes at a point when a great many of the family human are about to move into the final years of their current incarnation on the planet. Rather than be disappointed by such a thing, they can begin to put into practice what they have learned and gained in their time here.

In the past 300 years, the imbalance of yang energy on the planet manifested itself in warlike eras. Many perished in difficult and distressing ways. In the cycle of rebirth, those returning were given smaller lives to lead; that is, not all the energy of a previous life was brought together for the new earthly existence. This produced more humans but not necessarily strong ones. This is now coming to a conclusion. The majority of beings born today are more complete, more powerful, and more capable of gaining and promoting spiritual balance. Have you met them yet? Many are still infants.

What about You?

You are the elders of the tribes now. You have a measure of wisdom gained by years of experiences that no other humans in history have experienced! Think on this for just a moment. When in all of history has society changed so swiftly as in the past 100 years? When have so many people been able to speak their minds and open their hearts to such a wide audience? When has global communication been so instantaneous and accessible? Never before has the family human experienced such a massive growth spurt of the communication, or voice, chakra. This is only the beginning of how coming generations will exist. You, the people alive today, manifested all of these advances. You have set the stage for one of the greatest leaps of the family human.

Already you have gained much in your knowledge of the universe and solar system. This will continue at an increasing rate. The current adult population's participation in bearing witness to new discoveries is important. By making these facts and concepts a part of daily knowledge and reality, you set the pace for a new way of viewing the universe. Your manifestation of the future is not concluded. You are still at work on a level you are only beginning to realize.

This, then, is who you are now. You are finely trained beings with a legacy of creating the image of one world that is at peace and prosperous. Yet it remains an image to many. We tell you now that there is powerful reality behind the image, and many of you are living in such a way without fully noting this fact.

A small minority of beings persist in creating fear-based stories and dwell only on thoughts of chaos and entropy. They are loud and public at the moment, but they are only the remnants of such an energy. You can quell their restless nature. You can soothe this jagged nature. How can this be accomplished? Exert your peace. Go public with your vision for a peaceful planet. Speak of the current times of change in positive, growth-based language. Tell others of your view not in an argumentative way but rather in terms of possibility.

When faced with difficulties, too many people focus only on the immediate future of weeks or months. This focus is too narrow and does not allow for care and consideration. Instant decisions lead to short-term actions that result in choppy, messy answers to problems that require long-range solutions over years and even decades. The world society is moving very fast now. It is not always a benefit to have instant communication because it leaves little time to ponder or meditate. Often there is not even the opportunity to examine decisions in hindsight. Forcing issues and answers does not gain what is needed for the future. Because of this, society as you know it today is in a state of dismantling. This is not something to avoid. You can take some control. You can direct and guide the way many of the new beings think and act. This does not mean you will run for office or become great leaders of political activity. This is part of what is being dismantled. Why support the old ways?

How Do Things Look Now?

Spiritual concepts have gained mainstream attention. There are many who understand as reality what a few decades ago was thought of as occult. A few hundred years ago, these same things were thought of as heresy. Ponder this for a moment. Beliefs now common on all levels of society, including in science, mathematics, geography, history, and psychology, as well as through spiritual teachings, were once punishable by torture or death. The organizations and dogmatic systems that promoted such atrocious actions still exist today but are weakened. Speak clearly of your vision for a peaceful future of equality among all beings. Cast a bright light and remove these shadows from the fabric of the coming human society.

You have been tested by the fires of events that will soon be considered ancient history to the beings born in the next decades. You are stronger than you know, though many of you feel a deep weariness. Will the arguing among nations or ideologies never stop? Will people ever cease killing each other in the names of their gods? How can the chaotic nature of isolated, disenfranchised people be relaxed so that they no longer feel the need to destroy innocents at random?

These are the fires that remain. These are the first tests of purification facing the generations in schools now. Are they up to the challenge? Were you up to the challenge of your generation? Only time could tell, and the answer is yes, you were. You still are, but you need to see clearly who you are now and what your responsibility is to the planet and the beings living here in the future.

It is not up to the generation of advanced years to continue to press against the old patterns. You have worn them away, eroding the foundations past a point of return. Your constant pursuit of peace, your desire for increased joy, and your chant of love kept an energy of growth alive, nourishing it to maturity.

The energy that arises now, that rising tide, will further supply Earth and all beings with the strength to pursue these goals but in a different way. You are polished. You are skilled in imagining a new way. Continue and increase the reflection of spiritual qualities in every action you take. It is inherent within you. Release completely the old ways. Look at the coming years, and know that soon many will pass away from the planet. Help them to do so in a pain-free manner. Assist them in their journey from this phase of life. Accept what is a natural cycle.

There will be a time when the wave of energy will once again go to a low tide, though not as low as the past decades. Many of you will likely wash away from the planet at that time. It will be a more peaceful transition than people of previous centuries experienced.

A new wave will approach after that. The generation brought to Earth at that time will be the ones to feel the peace that you now imagine. They will be joyful for life and all it offers. Love will be an abiding principle of their daily routines. And in the cycle of life, death, and rebirth, there will be a strong energy of returning beings.

We say to all who read these words that there is power within you. Create a new path of conclusion for earthly life. It is not a cessation of life; it is a transition. Take joy in a life well lived. Love those who have brought you purifying lessons. Be at peace when the moment of transference comes. It is who you are now.

CHAPTER FOUR

Clarify Your Choices

As above, so below. On Earth today in the community of spiritually minded beings, there are often those who seek guidance. Many look outside of themselves for the answers to questions and to problems that arise. Often they look to those in the spirit realm for guidance. We gladly give it when needed. However, the time has come for people to act in a more self-sufficient manner.

You are capable of discerning the most energetically advantageous path for yourself without looking to your spirit guides. This does not mean that we are not here for you but that you can be more independent in your lives. The ability to make your own choices is a sign of spiritual maturity and strength.

Likewise, there is a need for the members of the family human to make strong social and intellectual choices. We in the spirit realm do not often take part in these matters. There are many questions being raised in communications between the physical and spiritual realms. Many are looking for absolute answers or very specific lines of action that will be the most optimal path to a peaceful, prosperous future. We offer this guidance to you now with the understanding that many of you are already aware of these concepts. Take these words as reminders.

In all phases of conscious existence, there are moments of choice. It should be clear that the beings on Earth face such a moment now. Each choice will create greater consequences for every other moment of choice that follows. The choices made by those alive on the planet today will affect future generations for many centuries.

There is a strong visible struggle between two forces on Earth. There is a compression of energies. What appears to be a struggle in the physical realm is in reality a coming together of energy. Knowing this does not make the times easier for the family human because there is much about this action that can create discomfort. What can people do for themselves at this juncture? How can the undivided, spiritually minded being act to alleviate pressure on him- or herself as well as for others?

Use Principles Rather Than Laws

There are guidelines for making appropriate spiritual choices. We choose to address some of these in broad terms. That in itself is a guideline. We in the realm of spirit will not lay down strict laws for you to follow. There are more principles in the conscious universe than there are laws. The closer one gets to gravity, the more laws are seen as unchangeable rules that, if violated, often result in a chaotic consequence. We offer a different perspective.

The energies that are coming together have never truly been apart; they are merely rebalancing. Change is imminent for the planet. We refer to these energies as yin and yang and have said before that yin is rising in strength. This is not a process that can be halted. It can be diverted or suppressed for a time, but the result will be that yin will rise. This is as close to a law as we will speak of at this time. Attempts to suppress yin will have the aforementioned chaotic consequences. We refer here to human society.

Using an ethical principle rather than an unbending law provides more flexibility. When you are dealing with things that exist only in the realm of gravity, it is good to know the laws that pertain to their activity. However, when dealing with conscious life, you will find that accepting variety and diversity will always serve you better as you seek to grow spiritually. You can maintain a strong, perhaps even strict, ethic while still allowing for diversity in others. Doing so will not alter your personal path. Many in these times seek to prevent others from following their own principles. They would prefer to impose their personal visions on others. As the energies compress, we will see great efforts made to gain control over others. These efforts may at first look beneficial, but they will soon prove to be an imbalanced action.

Be Aware of Areas of Weakness

How can such efforts be identified? Language is a key factor in becoming aware of who is actively supporting or suppressing yin. Yin energy is a peaceful, nurturing power. It is best served by yang energy when yang supports the growth that yin indicates. When people speak of a separation of yin and yang, as in yang being above or always the dominant energy, you can be sure that they are seeking to suppress yin.

Certain words are clues. The term "war," for example, is not a word that easily emerges from a yin-based society. In the physical realm of Earth, yin is primarily expressed through the feminine gender in nearly all species. There have been few women warriors in history. Those who have existed often were driven to war by actions taken against them, their families, or their tribes. Yin driven to violence is a fierce power and swift in its action. Yet yin will not carry a violent act beyond what is necessary. Most often, yin will seek to heal or negotiate. Yin seeks growth. Yin does not submit in meekness.

Those who freely utilize the term "war" or any variant that indicates strife and fighting or conflict are acting from an imbalanced yang. This form of yang is actually weak and seeks to gather many for an imagined cause in an effort to gain strength. These groups may divert the yin energy, but they will only hold one another down as yin rises above them. Eventually they will need to release their hold on their anger, or weak yang, and try to find the same level of peace that will be offered by the rise of the yin energy. Those who do not will witness the dissipation of their own energy as it fades from Earth.

Another way to identify the attempted suppression of yin is to note those who wish to remove choices from others. These people may offer high-minded speech regarding their reasons or appeal to a higher power, but the removal of choice from any being is a violation of that person's ability to create a self-directed karmic path.

The choices we refer to here are ones that do not directly affect others. Certain lifestyles or belief systems that are practiced in private or choices based on personal health or diet should not be interfered with. People who make such choices are taking full responsibility for their lives and are dealing with the consequences.

Some may attempt to label these choices as right or wrong. The universe does not deal with such concepts as right and wrong. It also does not mete out punishment. There are consequences, and that is all. If an action does not directly affect another being, then release any judgment about it and continue on your own karmic path.

Seeking to convert another to a way of life that would suppress or remove choice is also a clear indication of the suppression of yin as well as a sign of weakened yang. Strong yang is best expressed not through large dominating groups but through strong individual existence.

Strong People

How does one gain strength as an individual? It requires effort and action. In the same way as a physical being builds muscle through sustained effort and exercise, a strong individual is consistent in examining the world around him or her and gaining knowledge about it. That person would look at all things with a critical eye, seeking not to accept or reject a thought or concept but to gain a new perspective. The strong individual creates a sort of filter for him- or herself, allowing through only what creates true growth within. This filter is not so rigid as to let only preselected things pass. It is more of a membrane that recognizes elements that will serve the individual's progression along a personal path.

Although a strong individual may not allow certain elements to enter within the personal field, he or she also will not seek to stop others from accessing those elements. Such a person might discuss the benefits of a particular point of view but would not insist others change their minds.

An individual is an undivided being. People act on strong energies that are natural to the universe and specifically to Earth. Forcing others to act in a certain way is not a natural path. Following your own path when others take a different way is a sign of truly strong yang energy that is coupled with and led by truly strong yin. No conflicts arise out of such beings. Many conflicts are resolved because of those who have sought to strengthen themselves in this way.

The quest for one act that will create a peaceful and prosperous future is not a foolish thing. Understand that in asking, there is the strong energy of hope and the willingness to accept change. Understand too that there is no single rule or law that will make certain this eventuality.

Note the examples given, and observe how they reflect the search for peace through the avoidance of war and conflict. Note too how they allow for the principle of love to exist at many levels in each person in whatever way he or she chooses to express it. Finally, feel how the quality of individual balanced strength can bring a high level of joy to your life as you act on self-improvement and growth.

In these ways you — the individual, the undivided one — not only create a peaceful and prosperous life for yourself and those around you but also form the foundation of a future in which yin is supported by yang. In your doing so, all beings alive reap the benefits of a growth-oriented lifetime.

CHAPTER FIVE

Your Strength and Purity

As above, so below. In all levels of existence, there are opportunities for growth. As a spiritual being, you will seek a constant path of growth. It is clear that not all beings are on a pure, spiritual path, but growth and change are still offered to them. There are ways to increase the speed and strength of your growth. They have much to do with the concepts of body, mind, and spirit.

From the realm of spirit, we often ask humans to take actions that benefit them in a certain way. It appears that for the majority of humanity, taking action is not the preferred method of instituting change or growth. Many choose to react to circumstance rather than prepare themselves in recommended ways. While on the planet, the individual human reacts to various types of stimuli. The lower the vibration of the being, the more base the stimulus needs to be to elicit a reaction. For the majority of the family human, fear is now the primary stimulus that evokes a reaction. This is why there appears to be little spiritual growth happening in the world's population. Fear is the main form of energy that can not only prevent growth but also destroy life.

Toxins in the World

Of concern to many are the concepts of toxicity and purity. These ideas pertain primarily to the body, but the mind and the spiritual level of each person in the family human are considered to be at risk. It is easy to see that putting toxic substances into the physical form will cause growth to be hindered or altered in a detrimental way. Dangerous chemicals or radiation can seep into your life and, in quantity, prohibit a smooth progression.

In pursuit of profit and convenience, many food suppliers are using methods that some people believe are dangerous for human consumption, especially if exposure is prolonged. Movements are growing, and calls are being made demanding that the food producers cease using these methods.

The strongest proponent of growth for the human at any level is to make personal choices regarding his or her physical form. This is not to say that information you receive is in error. We are saying that you must think for yourself. Ask yourself, "Is this all the pertinent information necessary to make a decision?" Do not blindly react to fear-based claims. There may be truth in some of the words, and the decision to refuse to use certain products may be wise, but test these things out for yourself. Ask direct questions.

The human body is not so frail! You must remember that once humans did not have the knowledge of hygiene or the constant availability of fruits and vegetables, yet humanity survived and has thrived. Once there were many dangers in simple daily life and no hospitals or nurses to care for the injured and sick. Yet look now at the number of beings alive! The family human has arrived at this point after a long history of less-than-pure water and very rough food preparations. Of course, we do not say that a being should ingest polluted food or water. We say that there are many generations who survived many impurities and actually became stronger in many ways.

Where populations are dense, pollution and refuse are mounting problems with no easy solutions in sight. It is true that too many are clustered in certain areas. This will change. A balance will be achieved. But this is no reason to give in to fear-based reactions.

Pure Thought, Pure Emotion, Pure Spirit

Seek purity in all that you do, but do not forget that the body, as well as the earth itself, is a filter, one that purifies energy in ways you do not yet understand. This applies to the mind as well as the body. The emotions and the thought processes that together make up the mind also conduct a filtering process. It is clear that in these times, there is much to clog those filters. Again, we tell you to think and make wise decisions on the information you allow into your heart and head. Once damaged, these areas recover more slowly than the body. The body can heal a wound or disease. The heart and brain have memories that outlast the physical wounds.

A vast amount of useless information is available to a large number of people on Earth. Some of it is relatively harmless and even entertaining. It can be enjoyable and is often useful to the regeneration, and sometimes it even stimulates thought and emotion. But a great deal of this information is rhetorical and pretentious. Often, the purpose of this empty talk is to be divisive and self-inflating. We have said to you, "Do not waste your words." In this, we meant limit what you say to others regarding your spiritual growth. We reapply the phrase now to indicate that you not waste your thoughts with so many words.

Purify what you take into your senses. Allow personal thought and emotion to exist, and you will feel stronger. Press away what creates fear within you, and your growth will renew and continue. Only in this way will healing come to damaged hearts and brains.

Many of you desire spiritual growth and often place this as your highest goal. This is noble. We remind you now that you are not simply spirit beings. While on the planet, you are firmly in the physical realm. You must take care of your bodies as best as you can. This, then, is the core of spirituality while incarnate.

Of course, there is much more to spirituality than being healthy in body. Seeking and pursuing spiritual goals is necessary. Remaining centered and well balanced are primary indications of a spiritual being. This extends to having a productive physical life. Some people may sit back and wait for the spiritual realm to provide for them physically. This is not our responsibility. We assist in times of difficulty, true. But many beings never attempt to raise themselves out of difficult situations, or they act in ways that are irresponsible with what has been previously provided.

Energy is not limited, but the flow of energy can become restricted. If a channel is clogged, then it will be difficult to create a continuous stream of resources. It is in this way, then, that you can more clearly visualize the need for purity in your physical, mental, emotional, and spiritual aspects of life.

The Essence of Purity

Purity is not the absence of everything. Outer space is pure, but it is not hospitable for the family human. Water that has been cleansed too well has little to offer a plant in the way of nutrients. Certain challenges are built into life on the planet. When training for physical strength, you must put forth a steady effort of movement. When seeking knowledge, you likely submit to various tests on facts and reason to ensure you are on a steady course of intellectual growth. When pursuing a new emotional relationship, you exert your emotions and risk your heart in a flow directed outward to the other being.

Like a knife that is sharpened when drawn along a stone or wood that is polished with an abrasive surface, life is strengthened when allowed to brush up against things that challenge a being. Similarly, it is like what you feed your mind. You begin to think that what you see and hear is truth if it is untested by counterthoughts. Sharpen your mind and body by challenging yourself mentally and physically.

Even in spiritual life, growth is promoted by challenge. It is said that it is easy to be holy when isolated atop a mountain. To prove your spirituality to yourself, you must practice it in everyday existence: at your job, within your family, while you travel, and so on.

We do not tell you to seek huge, challenging situations. A strong being will be able to accept large challenges, but it is not wise to live on the edge of what is reasonable. Remember, one of the primary attributes of a spiritual being is to be peaceable. It is difficult to be at peace when you are in constant contest with the universe.

Too many challenges can weaken a being. You can become overwhelmed by circumstances if you are unprepared or not strong enough. Taking advantage of the little lessons is important. It is these times that will sharpen your abilities to deal with tangled energies.

Purity, then, has more to do with purpose than substance. Living a purified existence will often mean a simpler life, being content with less. In the current age, you will experience an ever-easier flow of information. In the near future, possesion of knowledge will become less inclined to the individual and more directed toward the collective consciouness. The meaning of this is not yet apparent to the masses, but those who are spiritually sharpening themselves are beginning to realize the implication of the term "oneness."

Purity is an energy that contributes to a healthy, balanced life. It is the removal of words and thoughts that are divisive. It is the application of personal decision making and the acceptance of responsibility for your body, thoughts, feelings, and spiritual connection.

Purity leads to strength. Strength leads to growth. Growth is seen in the levels of love, joy, and peace that you express in your daily life on Earth and in the midst of all other members of the family human. This is a planet of purification. Your part is your life. Refuse to react to fear and growth-destroying tendencies. Take action, and make your decisions.

CHAPTER SIX

Live in the Present to Create the Future

As above, so below. Life on Earth is a marvelous experience. It is unlike any other form of existence within the galaxy. Here, a concentration of diverse energies and a consciousness of will are present that have not been necessary in the universe for many eons.

The pattern of life varies as beings cycle from a pure energetic spiritual form into a physical existence and then back again. We have described this as filtering energy. It is vastly more complex than what you can know while you are in the vibrations of gravity. Yet you have been in the higher realm of spirit and so have a veiled understanding of the continuance of the karmic forces. You also recognize, as do nearly all forms of life in existence on Earth today, the amazing changes occurring in this small point of the galaxy. All these things can become jumbled in the human mind. Confusion can exist even within the most spiritually minded.

What do you remember? Which are actually true memories, that is, personal thoughts or perceptions that your mind have made part of your personal reality? Which are external memories that have been impressed on you? Which thoughts and fears in your mind are actually based on nothing but tales that others told?

The Point of Living

There is much about to change in the world. It is not an easy alteration. Many people are in a state of belief that will make the change and the subsequent growth much more difficult. It is time for each being on the planet to perform a self-examination in a fearless way. It is time for each of you to focus your thoughts and your emotions on the future.

We often speak of past, present, and future. Many of you are very interested in future events. We must first point out that you are often looking at the future as either an unrealistic dream or an inevitable reaction to the past. Neither is true. Before we speak of future events, let us talk of the present.

The present is where you live. In one sense, the present is all you have. You, as a physical being, are held to time by gravity. You cannot transcend this state without losing your purpose on the physical plane. We have said this before and want to remind you now: For most beings, it is no accident that they are in physical forms at this time. There is power to this existence, and the future depends on the wise and intentional use of that power.

Each moment is a precious thing. It is where your energy is; thus, it is where you are focused on your karmic path. This is why it is important for you to "live in the moment," as is often said in certain traditions. The less consciously focused you are, the more likely it is that your future will be unfocused. Distractions will overtake your centering abilities and reroute them. This is not to say that a being should be so intense that he or she fails to enjoy the moments of each day. To the contrary: A balanced being's focus will automatically include such things as rest and recreation. In a natural way, these things are as essential to the creation of the future as is the supplying of physical necessities, such as water or shelter. There is a cycle to everything, and that includes your personal moment-by-moment focus.

When you find yourself in a situation that shows no opportunity for forward movement, it is not necessary to seek an avenue of escape. Often, merely waiting patiently and observing the situation will present an opportunity for growth. It is important to place your attention on what is, and then image what you desire. Seeking to force a change or chafing at the inaction does not contribute to harmony.

All beings become aware of moments when they made poor choices or took actions that did not benefit others or themselves. A slight variation is when one being is upset by another being's actions after doing the same thing to him or her. If beings dwell on these moments, they are said to be living in the past. They pursue recriminations against themselves or each other. There is no power in looking back. There is only a lesson learned.

The Opportunity of Life

There is a myth that most of the family human has believed for far too long. In the spirit realm, we ponder why it carries so strongly, even to the edge of an age of bright enlightenment. There remains a common belief in many religions and societies that at birth each being is inherently guilty of sin. It is true that no being is born perfect. This does not mean all humanity is somehow wrong or broken. Your humanness is not an error.

Everyone is imbued with paths and talents that are different from one another. This is not to say that a person is predestined for a specific course. The opposite is true. Releasing the artificial limitations that have bound humanity from birth will have the widespread effect of opening future humans to develop skills of hope rather than fear.

When human children are conceived and then born, they have spread before them a vast expanse of opportunity to create, learn, and enjoy one of the most beautifully diverse places in the galaxy. There are few planets and places that offer a spectrum of creative achievement greater than the Gaian home of Earth. It is here that much of the future course of the galaxy pivots. Yet this cannot happen in the present condition of the planet nor in the present state of mind of the family human.

We have said before that you are not the pinnacle of creation. You are, however, a strong race of creatives. The energy available to each human is extremely strong. It often comes to you in a pure form. You need only to begin to focus your will, and the necessary components will begin to be revealed. We implore you now: Do not waste this energy at this time.

Change is occurring, and it could take place in a more rapid way upon the planet. The discord we witness today impedes this change. It is up to each individual to slow the days and intentionally focus his or her share of the creative energy of the universe.

We say the words that follow directly to you, and we ask that you listen with fresh ears: You are a creative being. You are capable of creating change in your life. You are a being who can create balance and peace. You are able to see the future in a way that is unfettered with old mythologies and false guilt. You are able to look back and remember what is the truth, what you know deep in your karmic core. You are able to see clearly what came before you arrived.

Remember now the clear, clean canvas that was spread out in front of you just before your entry into the physical realm. Is the life you are living what you intended at that time? Are the agreements you made then being met today? If the answer is no, it is never too late to take the appropriate creative action. It may not be an easy thing to alter your path. You may need to make sacrifices. Ask yourself now, "Is spiritual happiness better than what I currently possess? Can I imagine a life more centered and peaceful than the one I currently exist in? Is there a possibility that I may loosen the restrictions I have accepted?"

Many have done just so in the past twenty years, and more are beginning to awaken to the opportunity. We are not asking you to abandon everything that is and to run from problems. Rather, take that fearless look at your current incarnation, and begin to imagine a life free of such weight and attachment.

Focus Your Life

For every person who takes this step, a chain of actions will begin that benefits the planet in the future. Every being who seeks to balance him- or herself in all ways on the physical plane will contribute to balancing the societies that are in existence. For every being who releases an old boundary that is meaningless on today's Earth and replaces that ancient border with a vision of understanding, the peaceful nature of the planet will manifest swiftly in that physical location. For every opportunity taken to reach out and adjust the perception of the world from one of good versus evil to the true vision of natural creation and enjoyment of all life, the planet gains an expanding element of joy. For every being who focuses on love rather than accepting false calls for fear and hate, the planet will settle into a sector of growth and cooperative prosperity.

The focus you need to make is not on others directly. It is on yourself and your inner attitudes. The old beliefs do not work. They have never truly been beneficial in a long-term sense. The new way, acceptance of others and the support of all levels of life, will wash away those ancient myths of evil.

There is no one and nothing in the realm of spirit that is trying to destroy you. There are many who wish you success and prosperity. You are we. We extend to you now this reminder of love: It is a pivotal time, and we ask that you imagine and focus on the concept of an Earth with many diverse beings who exist in harmony and growth. Your action counts. Focus your love.

CHAPTER SEVEN

Be Attached to Earth

As above, so below. A time of testing is upon us all, for both those incarnate and those in the lower spaces of the spiritual realm. We are in a period of shifting energies, and gravity affects us and our existence. Your immediate spiritual companions are close to you now. It is fair to say that we are closer to you than at any time in the past 6,000 years. We will become closer still in the coming years.

There can be little doubt that the planet is fluctuating and shifting, and the societies on Earth are also in a troubled and shifting time. When the earth literally goes through motions, such as earthquakes or strong storms, many things are pulled down and left in an unusable state. Do you feel as if you are facing similar experiences in your personal life?

These are not times for fear. Rather, they are times for greater awareness. Are you steadily increasing your awareness of things that matter, or are you seeking to distract yourself in the hopes that all things will simply work themselves out? Do you believe that institutions of finance, faith, government, and political power will return to a previous path? They will not. What will replace these long-standing organizations? Much of the answer to that question is up to you.

Earth and You

The simple fact is that, while incarnate, you are of the earth. You are of the elements of the planet and subsequently are ruled by the same laws of science that rule all matter. You are still learning about those rules, and as such, you still tend to react to situations like other life forms do. The idea that matter can be manipulated in ways undiscovered is a difficult thought that sounds like magic or fantasy. Yet certain segments of the science community are realizing just such a concept: Mere presence can affect outcome.

Are you present in your life? Are you actively affecting the outcome of your life in ways that benefit you and others around you? This would mean that you are not reacting to situations and events but are taking a proactive approach.

It begins deep in your thoughts and feelings. Thought is often necessary to gain a desired outcome, but emotion and desire are vital. Through them, you create an image of what you want without a need to know how the goal will be achieved. If you spend too much time in thought and logic, you will find that you are striving to sequence events in a specific fashion. This narrows the potentials for how your desire is achieved. It is better to allow the Source energy of the universe to act in the most natural way and to let your goal be achieved in a state of harmony. Logic will always adjust a concept downward, seeking to make things more efficient and compact. Emotion and desire will always create space for abundant results.

There are moments in an earthly life that take on profound significance. These are times when greater amounts of energy are received or released. From a karmic perspective, these periods appear to be spirals or what some may term as chakras or vortexes. Do you fully comprehend the concept of energy centers? They are all around you and also within you! Awareness of these energy centers, especially those within, will assist you in navigating the constant changes that occur. Particularly in these days of increased and substantial changes, it is good to sharpen your personal vision to observe the energies that affect you. This skill will allow you to more productively affect the energies of life and the future in a growth-oriented way.

The vortexes of Earth have shifted and continue to do so quite dramatically. Animals are adapting naturally to this activity, though it may take several generations to fully acclimate. The family human is the sole species resisting these energetic alterations. Of course, not all of humanity is resisting, but those of you who are spiritually aware can clearly see that a vocal faction seeks a return of old pathways and old belief systems. You cannot return to the ways of the ancient herders and wanderers. You have become too intelligent to believe in spiteful, vengeful deities.

It is true that a more pastoral age is near. This does not mean, however, that there will be a return of ancient superstitions and sacrifices. This will be an era of great harmony for all life forms. The earth itself will adjust your vibration, and the family human that exists at that time will respond with a high level of joy. The enhancement of life will correspond with the stabilizing of the energetic vortices, the chakras of the planet, and all life on it. You will truly comprehend that you are of the earth and are also its stewards rather than its owners.

You can feel a measure of this new age today by consciously releasing old patterns and expectations. You must cease looking to the past and focus on the present as the first step into the future. Only you can write your energetic legacy. What will you give to the future?

The Evolution of Life

The evolution of all species is marked by moments of decision. This is not to say that all species have a conscious thought process, logically weighing all options and selecting the best genetic alteration. Rather, the decision is one created by the circumstances of changing energy. Every great evolutionary leap is accompanied by powerful energetic changes of Earth.

For the first time, one species has the opportunity to directly influence the changes that will come not simply for themselves but for many other species. Is it surprising that so many are concerned with the rights of animals? The care of the environment, in an effort to protect habitats for a variety of species, has taken on a consistent energy. The mass resistance to exploitation of earthly resources is new, and it is a significant aspect of the path of the new human, those we call the children of the Sun.

We are not saying that you should involve yourselves in protest efforts or spend your personal resources and energy pursuing dramatic, instantaneous change. This is unnatural. Changes take place in specific patterns in the realm of gravity. Forcing change will alter the sequence and potentially delay the exchange of one energetic pattern for another. Avoid mass hysteria.

Do what you can on a personal level or in a community-based effort. Create observable results on a small scale, and in this way, you create patterns for the future. Act consciously. Do not judge what exists. Seek to optimize the future through small, intelligent activities. Recall that change is constant. Understand that evolution is occurring as you take in these words.

Release Yourself from Earth

Are you cognizant that all life is a cycle? Do you pay attention to the time passing? This is not meant to place urgency in your perspective. Rather, it is meant to bring the passages of history into your view. You live in a time of momentous events. What occurs now can set the future on a different course. Are you actively participating, or do you only seek a time when you will exist in a different realm? Do you envision the spirit realm as one of only pleasure and leisure? The realm of spirit is an active one with many paths and responsibilities to occupy a being! There will be time enough to follow those ways when you arrive. Your focus should be on your current existence and the effect you can create for the future.

Understand that the time of your passing is an important event for your karmic entity. Prepare yourself for this by living joyfully in the present. Prepare those around you to celebrate the ending of an incarnation and to let your energies move on. Monuments of stone and sealing of the elements of the body are not natural ways. These are things that will create gravity about the energies that are released from the physical form. Do you wish to remain partially on the planet?

Many struggle to overcome the pull back to Earth after they have transitioned from the planet. For some, part of their initial contract is to remain as a type of energy here on Earth. These exceptional beings are few. The energies of those who have gained fame through charitable activities, art, or entertainment can adhere to memorials created in their honor. Separating their energies from the earth takes a greater amount of time.

Many other beings are caught between realms because their loved ones seek to honor them by erecting physically significant memorials. A better memorial is to commit one's life to greater love and peace. Would you wish that those remaining on the planet after you leave act in positive ways rather than waste time and resources on inert statuary or markers? This also applies to the passing of animal companions. Release all the valuable resources and energy. Do not remain attached to the earth longer than necessary. You will return soon enough.

Make a decision now to pass from this life with a measure of joy. Do not seek to be remembered; instead, work to leave an energetic legacy. Living today in a peaceful and loving way will assist you in this endeavor. Envision the life you wish for future generations. Act as if that is the way of life in the present. Doing this will allow you to actively participate in your return to the realm of spirit, minimizing the transition time from the lower vibrations of gravity into the higher-vibrational existence you seek. It will then allow you to return to the planet, to reincarnate, at a higher vibrational level. You will reenter the earthly realm and witness a planet of great peace and harmony. The beings living here will have ample opportunity to express joy. It is a place you will love. Can you imagine this now? Act as if it is here!

CHAPTER EIGHT

Your Perfect Core Energy

As above, so below. The universe is energy. All life is energy. Energy cannot be destroyed; it can only be transformed. In this sense, there is no such thing as death. There is transformation from one type of energetic existence into another. What you currently feel as life is a continuation of energies that have existed since Source began to express itself in a physical way. Yet from the vantage point of a spiritually aware member of the family human, life is more than just a series of energetic exchanges or alterations. At your core, you sense that you are more than simple energy. This awareness demonstrates clearly that you possess a higher state of consciousness.

The Challenge of Becoming Balanced

Existence is tangible, and you can be aware of it on many levels. When beings become incarnate on the planet, awareness arrives in several phases. Consciously, the individual human is first aware of him- or herself as a physical entity. As an incarnation progresses, you become more emotionally and then mentally cognizant. Interestingly, at the instant of birth, most humans are more spiritually complete than at any other time during the rest of their incarnation. It is the point of life when you remain the most unaffected by the physical realm of gravity. Even within the womb throughout gestation, you are shielded from the effects of the realm of gravity in many ways. The connection to your karmic thread maintains a clarity not easily accessible after your physical arrival and separation from your mother.

It is only after the process of birth that you are directly affected by the world. You then build your personal experiences and perceptions without the filtering protection of belonging to another life form, that of your mother. From that point, you develop an identity that is entwined with other beings.

The purity of your karmic essence fades. That karmic essence is never lost, but as you progress through life on the planet, there are many disruptions and distractions to your true spiritual nature.

All events that occur around you may have a greater or lesser meaning, and each adds to your personal experience. However, there is little that directly points you to spiritual satisfaction. This must come from within you rather than from outside. There may be examples of a spiritual path or teachers who possess certain skills and knowledge, but the true spiritual being must eventually find his or her own way. This is not easy, especially in the past several centuries. There is much about the societies on Earth that is imbalanced. Any and all imbalances of energy that have occurred on the planet affect your life course, and, despite your best efforts, you will often find yourself thrown off center. There is purpose in this system, but it is not easy to navigate.

Follow the Example of the Universe to Gain Balance

The universe is in perpetual motion. Change is constant. Energies radiate out from unnumbered actions, creating further interactions that spread change even further. To and fro, one thing affects others, which then continue the process.

While on Earth, you may easily see this principle in your interactions with other members of the family human. In your closest dealings, you can perceive how others can sway you from your center. It is inevitable that balance will be lost, especially during times of mental or emotional crisis.

The spiraling motion of the universe is set to create balance, although not always in the way you would perceive it from the vantage point of life on Earth. The core energetic activity of the family human emulates this universal motion, but there is a difference. It is not simple subatomic charges spinning and whirling. You possess a consciousness, a decision-making energy, that allows you to choose a different path from one that might seem easy or obvious or even inevitable.

This, then, is a part of the key to understanding the experiment of life on Earth. There is more to it than making conscious, long-range, thoughtful choices. First, understand that there is no such thing as impure energy. All energy is pure at its core. It carries no judgment or motivation. Energy only seeks to express creativity. This is in alignment with the Source energy of all things. When this creative purpose is deflected or delayed, there is imbalance.

In the life of a human, imbalance takes the emotional shape of frustration or disappointment. Expression of these emotions will bring a continuance of the same type of reactions, increasing their intensity.

A sense of anger or a lack of happiness is not a mistake or flaw; it is a signal of internal imbalance. These emotional reactions often occur when you have been looking outside of yourself for balance. Here, then, is the choice point: By acknowledging your own energetic imbalance, you now can choose a different action. You now have an opportunity to rebalance your energy in conscious awareness. By releasing your connection to a specific outcome from any other being or external force, you set into motion a chain of balancing actions.

It is sometimes easier to achieve a form of balance by avoiding attachment to other people or even society. A solitary existence, by its very nature, is one in which the isolated human cannot often be affected by outside energies. Many disciplines have some form of monastic or solitary living as part of their spiritual questing. Some systems of belief recommend detachment from all things. Is this necessary? It is true that a simpler life can yield more time for contemplation. Does this serve you and the rest of the planet? To some extent it can. By your example, you may direct others to a similarly simple life. However, the rest of the physical universe does not possess a clear model for such a solitary existence.

There are constant interactions of gravity, magnetism, and many other forces, some yet unknown to the family human. Throughout the universe, the maintenance of balance in the face of all these energies is a beautiful dance of spirals and spinning. A life fully lived on Earth will seek engagement with other energies. This reflects the complex universe.

You can and will encounter powers that shift you from your core energy. The stronger your personal gravity, the less likely you are to be thrown far off balance. Here is where we see the beauty in the dance. The establishment of a coordinated circling with others creates a larger centering force. This is another key to comprehending the experiment of life on Earth.

The entwining of energy into a larger, balanced form is a vital aspect of life on the planet. Here we must tell you that it is more accurate to say life "with" the planet, and this is why we refer to planet Earth as Gaia, for that is the name of the life force that exists within the very core of the physical Earth. In the same way that you are a karmic consciousness manifest in a physical form, Earth is the physical form for the ever-maturing consciousness commonly called Gaia.

Create a Higher-Vibrational Life from Your Core Energy

In the matter of Earth's consciousness, the expression of the term "Gaia" is one that was chosen. There is deep power within that name, and that power is increasing. It is currently in a strong state of rebalancing. You can be an important continuance of that power by choosing a balanced approach to your core energy. As Gaia balances herself, your core energy responds. Seeking appropriate balance puts you in increased harmony with your chosen home planet.

Earth is filled with cycles of symbiotic life. The consciousness of Gaia is rising, and you are gaining an opportunity to rise along with this creative being. This is a physical process in many ways and a true spiritual action as well. The more you create joy and happiness, especially within yourself, the closer your connection to a higher-vibrational future will be. The more peace you radiate, the more you alleviate the pain and imbalances of the past. The stronger the sense of love that you emanate, the more powerful your own present moments will become. This then creates an opportunity for others to also become empowered by joy and peace and love.

You are the same energy as the rest of the universe. All energy comes from the Source of all things. It is pure and awaiting creative opportunities. At the core of your being exists perfectly balanced energy. Choosing a creative path, one that makes you consciously happy and brings joy, propels and strengthens the purity of the Source energy that resides within you. Seek to create peace and joy deep within yourself. Choose to consciously express love, and your core will align with the core energies of Source.

CHAPTER NINE

Create a Spiritual Life

As above, so below. Are you seeking to increase your inner balance in a troubling society? Are you looking ahead in your life to gain a higher level of existence? Do you wish to manifest a keener sense of spiritual energy?

Many people today have an acute sense that they are part of something larger, that they possess a higher purpose. It is easy to connect with that higher self when thinking of the future and a common eventuality that faces all humanity. However, we are not speaking of that transition from the physical realm back into spirit. We are asking you about this current incarnation of yours.

It is important to remember that there is much that can and should be accomplished in the present. No matter your belief system, you can see that you have a strong presence on the planet at this moment. By paying closer attention to the here and now, you will gain much in the search for increased spirituality.

How to Create a Practical Path of Spiritual Growth

It is easy and common for people to get caught up in speculating what comes after physical death. After this life, things will run a natural course. There is very little you need or are able to control from the realm of gravity.

There is little that can be controlled throughout the universe. Much of the activity that occurs simply does not need a consciousness to affect it. Planet Earth is unique in many ways. Here, there is a collection of consciousness, and you are a distinct and individual part of that consciousness. This is not to indicate that there are no other beings of consciousness in the physical universe. Far from it. However, in most other instances, consciousness takes on a different form. It is less individualistic and more communal.

One of the factors that makes planet Earth unique is the ability of conscious beings like you to choose balance or imbalance in each incarnation. It is not a predestined thing for people to gain a higher vibrational level in the course of a single lifetime. However, by not making a conscious step toward this state, a being is in fact choosing to remain at a low level of existence. Gaia is on a course of spiritual increase, and in this way, all life will eventually attain such a higher vibration. It is better to be in harmony with Gaia and seek to raise your own vibration by choice.

The family human is gifted with a specific style of life. You possess both an emotional aspect and a logical aspect. From the perspective of the spirit realm, we often stress following the emotional aspect first and letting the logical powers structure this desire. However, if your desire is to gain a higher level of spirituality, increasing your connection with creative energies of Source, then you must begin to allow for a practical nature to affect that spirituality. You must let the path to the desire be structured.

Thoughts are powerful. When expressed in words, they take on a life of their own. All life on Earth is symbiotic with the planet. Creating thoughts that are beneficial for all other life on the planet increases the power and potential of the concept's becoming reality in the realm of gravity. In this way, manifesting what you desire can and will occur.

You may already see that truly spiritual beings rarely lack what they need in a physical sense. They appear to be taken care of and provided for as needs arise. This is a simple law of the universe. Plants and animals are good examples of this. All they need is available. It is true that at times there is an imbalance in Earth's energy. Weather patterns shift, droughts occur, and rivers overflow and flood the land. In each of these situations, it may appear as if plants and animals are not provided for, but these are points of rebalance. Most often the birds and mammals will migrate away from affected areas to places of supply. They make an effort. Effort is required even when provision is easy. In the same way, effort is necessary to gain and maintain your individual spiritual balance. We remind you now that you are of the earth. Any action taken on your part to increase your energies must be balanced between the physical, mental, emotional, and spiritual elements that make up your being.

Three Simple Phrases to Activate Your Spiritual Power

A spiritual being can and should remain firmly grounded when in the physical realm. They can acquire what is necessary for a comfortable life without sacrificing spiritual values. There are three principles that we often refer to that are adaptable to this course. For the purpose of manifesting, each of these principles can be expressed in simple statements that engage their power directly with your individual core levels of energy. It will be helpful for you to speak these phrases out loud.

First say, **"It is."** This is the power of acceptance of a situation. It becomes the recognition that things are a certain way. This does not lock the current energy into a specific place. It only gives you the awareness of reality. It is where you are and thus is your starting point for movement and activity. Choices made from reality are always more successful than choices made from a false sense of self.

What do you wish to change or adapt? Is your health less than optimal? Is your place of dwelling inadequate in some way? Is your emotional life unfulfilling? Are your thought patterns weak, or are you caught in a cycle of dwelling on elements of life that are unhappy or destructive? Only by taking a full and honest appraisal of your heart and brain will you be able to see clearly what is necessary for motion toward a higher vibrational and thus more satisfying lifestyle.

Saying, "It is," is an acknowledgment of place. It is not a commitment to remaining in place.

Second, combining that phrase with **"What next?"** will activate you and bring you closer in harmony with the natural flow of source energies. "What next?" is an activation of the imagination. Of course, to be successful in this, you must be realistic in what you image. Yet do not limit the scope too early in the process. It is good to have a wider picture of where you want to be in life. It is also wise to understand that these journeys occur in steps more often than leaps. By asking this question, you engage both heart and brain. We remind you now to begin with your heart's desire and allow the brain to structure the steps necessary to achieve the image.

The third phrase to invoke is, **"I am."** It is good to make this a reasoned statement, one of realism and process. These are the words of creation. "I am" is the closest thing to a name that Source energy has, and it remains the most powerful tool for creation that is available to all humans and other conscious beings. It is also the most misused of statements. All too often, people will say the words "I am" and then apply some ailment ("I am sick") or fear ("I am worried about money"), or they fail to finish the statement. This does nothing to move them forward. It allows things to remain the same and thus strengthens times of fear or lack. It is better to state, "I am healthy, vital, prospering, and happy." This, even if you do not feel strongly that these are true at the time, will begin to loosen the energies that prevent improvement and motion.

Accepting your current situation is not the same as agreeing that you should remain in such a state. Questioning a next step is not the same as indecision. Making a statement of fact when you are in fact not yet there is not simply dreaming. These are all activating phrases, and effort will still be required on your part. Using these phrases will place you in a beginning state of flow. It is a decisive moment when you begin this process. It is also a unifying moment. You may become aware of imbalances in your heart or brain, one side hindering the other. It is necessary to face these imbalances and, using the same three phrases, move yourself into a state of internal harmony.

Using your mind — that is, the heart and the brain working together — you can bring the energy of provision and manifestation to you easily. When the strength of logic supports the power of emotion, a strong wave of energy begins. This is yang supporting yin. Soon, motion will occur seemingly without effort. Of course, each of the three steps must be practiced, and balance in each phase must be maintained. This is where individual choice occurs. It is a continual process, not merely a one-time action. This is a path to increasing your spiritual nature. This path does not have an end.

Each phrase given to you here represents a personal adaptation of the three primary spiritual energies available to all conscious beings. The phrase "It is" is acceptance and is an aspect of peace. Asking the question, "What next?" ignites the imagination, which is an aspect of joy. Stating, "I am," and filling in the sentence with a powerful positive thought is creative in nature and a strong representation of Source energy and thus the spiritual energy of love.

Using these phrases, beginning now, will alter your perception and increase your ability to transform. The sense of peace may not be immediate, but when coupled with the feeling of joy that can come when you begin creating the life you truly desire, that peace will flow not just toward you but also through your entire life. In a short time, you will be able to say, "My life is peaceful. Every new day is joyful. I am a loving and loved being."

CHAPTER TEN

Walk Between the Ages

As above, so below. It is said that those now alive are the beings who walk between ages. That is a true statement, and those beings are you! What is the new age that is arriving? How does this differ from what came before? Why is there a demarcation from one period to another?

We will tell you of things future and past. The current energies you are experiencing now, those that are troubling to many people, are separating what was and what will be. The world society is in a deep stage of uncertainty. There is less to cling to in the present than ever before. If you feel adrift, you are clear in your perception, but this is not a time to feel dismay. It is a time to seek the new currents. Do not try to regain old riverbanks; they have washed away. Seek new shores. From the level of perception of the physical realm, these shores may appear distant, but from our higher perspective of the spiritual realm, we can assure you that they are closer than you imagine. Expand your imaginative powers now. There is much creative energy adrift with you!

Where You Are

You have now reached the end of false markers. You have passed artificial dates and boundaries that were used by some to create fear. It is true that some markers were important and real, but the ideas of calamitous endings and destructive judgments no longer have any points of time to cling to or get caught on. You are now free from ancient prophecies that were, at best, misunderstood by the masses.

Spiritually minded people are asking, "What now? What should my path into the future be? What should my life look like, and where do I now focus my attention?" The answers to those questions have not changed much from the past. The difference is that humanity once looked to specific events, moments that were noted and predicted from ages past. Expectations were placed on those dates. Many, even those with strong spiritual energy, believed that unrealistic, cataclysmic events would dramatically alter the world. Great changes did occur, and the effects of these days will continue and echo for some decades. Dramatic destruction is unnecessary to complete these changes.

The future is wide and unwritten. Apocalyptic timelines have expired. There are no clear prophetic dates remaining. The future has no such clear demarcations to become entangled in. We say this to you but also remind you that the energy of fear will continue for a short time. Just the fact that there is nothing recognizable ahead to dictate a path will frighten many of the beings trying to hold on to the old energies. To them, it is like looking over the edge of a precipice.

To spiritually minded people, this vision of the future is like a clean canvas prepared for a new artistic creation or a fresh page of paper ready for new words of wisdom. To this end, the old pages and what may once have been wisdom need to be set aside. We cannot emphasize this enough. What was once wisdom now is mere history and not very clear history at that. We will tell you some of the true history here, but it is more important to step away from these old things and gain a wider and higher perspective. Breathe fresh air and not dust.

Open to New Paths

You are not without guidance. The family human has never been without guidance from the spiritual realm. Now the family human is different. You have grown. You are expected to act with spiritual maturity and consciousness toward the future generations. The generations that have walked between worlds are also the generations that opened the way for a new kind of evolution. We are speaking about the generation currently in mature years.

A newer and more persistent energy is on the rise. This will create more opportunities for life to once again diversify. As in the past, this diversification will have its origins on Earth. Much attention will become focused on what is around Earth and within the influence of the central star. A time is approaching when those who live on Earth will experience a great expansion of their vision of the universe.

Shallowness of society and idle pursuits will be replaced with depth and the quest to expand knowledge and gain wisdom. Those who are willing to go deep on many levels will be the ones who thrive. A curious and questioning being is the hallmark of the new wave of humanity. What once seemed like magic is now reality. What makes you believe that this concept will not alter?

Avoid Pitfalls

You, as a class of humans, will be remembered for what you have survived. Many will be remembered as having altered the viewpoint of all humanity. Some of you will be noted for your direct efforts on behalf of all humankind. However, do not seek recognition.

Take right actions. Do that which is right to all that you meet, but do not seek a reward. A path of service is not one that receives direct physical recompense. There are those who have set themselves up as spiritual leaders. Some fail in this when their leadership becomes a thing others rely on over their own free will. A true spiritual leader does not collect tribute from followers. A true spiritual leader will direct fellow spiritual travelers toward attaining balance and radiating a clear and pure energy of peace. Each person will find and travel his or her own path.

The spiritual guidance that you might seek is no longer the domain of those who have studied long. It is intrinsic within each human. You are spiritually stronger now than even fifty years ago. Today, you are more capable of receiving and clearly comprehending information arriving from higher vibrational beings. Those who are born today carry this energy strongly, but they need to walk into a more balanced world than currently exists. The less time they must spend correcting the errors of false leadership, the sooner the planet achieves the goals that the current generations seek. Your goal remains this: Balance yourself, and in so doing, balance the energy of the family human. Some are saddened by this thought. Many were waiting to be rescued from imbalanced lives. Rather than to take action to change their present circumstances, people have been taught that only in the future would they find happiness.

The current generation, those who walk between the ages, will not be on the physical plane to witness the harvest of their efforts. Some have carried an expectation that there would be a reward for them in the present day. We tell you now, the best reward for the work you have done is the work itself. What you will experience in the future of your karmic line will make all that has gone before worthwhile.

There once was a path for all true spiritual leaders. In the distant and unrecorded past, those with true leadership abilities gained clear visions of the future and described these in detail. All of society then worked for future harvest and growth. The ability to have clear visions has been blocked for some time now. As a society, humanity is currently very shortsighted, looking only to what they might quickly gain and ignoring the cost to others. In the past, no one sought fame and the accompanying fortune of material goods. Celebrity is an empty, false energy. It does not nurture or nourish.

Release and Relief

Old ways will be left behind. We repeat: Those who seek to cling to the old energy will find themselves diminished. Many of the challenges of the future will come from the fear that these ones feel and create. The task of the new energy, and of those who seek to nurture and grow by it, will be to increase awareness of life's potentials. Pressure to conform will begin to relax. Those who are soft in their ways will dissipate. Those who are hard in their manner will break. Those who are supple will have easier access to the flow of energy that approaches Earth.

The focus on the past must and will shift. Those in the present spend far too much energy in recall and memory. Those who have died do not need continual honor. Their energy has regenerated into something other than what they were. Resources and time spent on people who are no longer alive would be better used on those who are approaching the planet.

Plenty of healthy activity is available. Walk away from contentious behavior. Support only the energy that allows for a growth of peace and equality among other beings. Exercise your own energy of love to others, and observe how disagreements slip away. Your joy in life will be enhanced when you release the need for outside validation. At all times, ask yourself, "Am I limiting my own joy of life through seeking power or the desire to gain favorable judgment?" Releasing judgment will do more for the future generations than you can imagine. Place your focus on the areas ahead. Create the new paths that others can walk. Today, right now, express love toward someone. Relax your heart and release love in all directions, especially toward the future.

CHAPTER ELEVEN

Your Path Ahead

As above, so below. You find balance in motion; you know stability in movement. People seeking peace must take proper action.

We approach you with these concepts that, at first, you may find simple. Although the universe is ultimately made of such simple thoughts and energies, all things act on all other things, especially within the realm of gravity. Actions of one thing affect others that are nearby. Each action creates new and increasingly complex reactions. We are at the most intricate moment in the stream of time in eons.

All things move in curving ways. If you examine the motion of all mass, you will find that a spiral is the best description of the basic structure of universal movement. You will note that, even within things growing on the earth, the spiral appears in a continual, specific ratio. You may, at times, believe that something is a straight line. We tell you now that the concept of the straight line is an illusion in most cases. It is a useful tool in measurement, but few things travel that way. To do so would be to exceed the power of universal gravity. Anything that defied this core principle of the physical universe would bring a catastrophic effect to the space-time continuum.

Right now, you might feel that you are in stillness. Yet this is a relative perception. You exist on Earth, which spins and tilts about the Sun. The Sun in turn also spins and tilts but at the same time is moving in a macro-orbital path about a galactic core. This core is ultimately in a vast cosmic dance with other galaxies, and they all act upon one another.

Earth's fellow planets all follow the Sun in an intricate, multilevel spiraling along its path. Periodically, the solar system is pulled and warped by gravity wells that it encounters along its journey. There are other forces that orbit the Sun, but at such distance, you have not realized their size or nature yet.

You can truly begin to comprehend that stillness is not a thing that a being on the planet can achieve. Yet you feel still, and perception becomes your reality. We speak of these things now so that you will understand what is to come.

The Coil of Time

Around the solar system and beyond, the coil of time has been pulled taut in recent decades. Indeed, it has been tightening for several centuries. Only in recent years has the entire planet felt this intensity of gravity and proximity. All things in space and time were pressing against all other things. Much has been achieved in this time, but much also has been crushed and removed.

Some are now becoming conscious of a flowing sense of opening, a release of pressure on many people and situations. There will still be chaotic action for a short time, but many are finding purpose and direction in the aftermath. Within the family human, there is a robust ability to create hope. From the realm of spirit, we encourage and strive to stimulate this feeling of hope within you all now. Despair does not serve the motion we seek to achieve. Hope will allow direction and unity of spirit on the planet.

We tell you now that the coil of time is still wound tightly. The opening and releasing of tension you may have recently noted or felt is like a warm day in winter. It is not actual spring weather. The tilt of the planet is still away from the Sun, and the colder days will likely return, but for that one day, the clouds part, the wind stills, and the air dries out, giving a temporary respite from harsher conditions. You enjoy the moment and draw strength for the near future. This respite from the tension of time is just that, a moment to regain balance and correct course.

A Completion of Contracts

The family human has come far in recent centuries. Now there is greater hope for the future, both near and far. What direction do you wish to go? What results do you wish to achieve in coming years?

We often speak of "contracts" being made for a person's specific incarnation. Their karmic thread brings them to certain situations that may echo past tragedy or pain, and their contract is to find a higher vibrational path through this life. In the past, these contracts often continued until that physical life was completed. The recent generations have been different.

Contracts have been completed and new ones arranged, sometimes several times within one lifetime. This has been possible because of the proximity we all have existed in during the tightening of the coils of time. This process will continue for a while yet, but there is something new in the arrangement. A great many contracts have concluded. There is a dwindling of unresolved energy from the past. Much of the family human is poised to make a leap forward, unencumbered by the residual karmic debts of past lives. The future now begins to open for new ways of creativity.

Much that has gone before is now at a great distance from the family human. You have passed many dense moments of gravity. All these things have affected you, whether you were alive for the events or not. All these things have influenced the paths of your lives. Today, you may see that much is behind you. The filtering of Gaia and her vitality is in vigorous motion, and we in the spirit realm witness many successes. Yet there is still much ahead.

What Approaches You, You Also Approach

The solar system now moves toward new encounters, and discoveries await. You are soon to receive information about your solar home and surrounding neighborhood that will alter the perceptions of those who will make up the next generations. Some alive now will continue to deny certain possibilities or facts. They will cling to ancient fables. The truly spiritually minded being is not one to fall prey to old fears. Source energy is creative by nature. It does not punish or destroy. Source energy does not sit in judgment. Keep this thought close to your hearts in coming days. There is still much to be filtered out and away from Earth, but now it is inevitable. The coils of time will soon relax enough for there to be no purchase hold for old energies.

What approaches does so with intent. There are other consciousnesses in the grand scale of the universe. They are near you now in a dimensional way. You are nearing each other on the physical plane, but this will take more time. There will be some continuing chaotic pressure as Gaia shakes off the remnant of what she has passed through. This is not a sign of destruction but of cleansing. The spiraling nature of her movement in concordance with her star and brother and sister planets is due to be more relaxed and less affected by strong gravity wells in this next segment of the galaxy. A cleaner, smoother road is ahead. Most of you will begin to feel this in your lives.

As you traverse the path of the Sun through the galaxy, you too can create intent for your future encounters. Imagine possibilities that are favorable to Gaia in the future. Consider the concept of synergy as you ponder and meditate and set your intention. In this, you set energetic goals and course corrections for yourself.

We ask you now to imagine a spiral. Think of it as a compressed spring. Meditate on the sense of pressure the coils feel. In your mind, allow the spring to relax slowly so as not to fly away. Feel the tension fade. Return to this image when you feel stress returning to your form or when you wish to make a choice regarding a direction for your life. A higher purpose has been calling all life on Gaia for some time now. It is becoming increasingly attainable to create foundations for the future for this higher quality.

Degradation of motion creates imbalance. Stopping movement causes instability. The proper action for seekers of peace is a continuance of hope. Kindle hope by expressing love for all beings. The expression of love grows when you experience joy at existence. Joy is amplified by appropriate actions.

CHAPTER TWELVE

Purify the Current of Time

As above, so below. These are important times, momentous in the course of history that is both recorded and unrevealed. Increased awareness is vital. We often give words of hope and encouragement, thoughts to feed and sustain spiritual seekers and sustain them on what can be a most difficult path. We remind you that there is little difference in the desires between those existing on the physical plane who follow a spiritual path and the beings who dwell in the realm of spirit. All of us wish for peace and abundance. All wish for the ability to express our creative natures. All wish to see balance return to the planet.

Seekers in the realm of gravity might feel as if they are a minority. It may seem as if many members of the family human do not desire such things. There are more humans in line with these desires than you know or can see. A variety of divisive factions of beings who attempt to cling to old ways gives the illusion of numbers. Still, they make a great deal of noise, and this can be a distraction.

Let us take a moment to illustrate how best to navigate your lives in this time.

The River

In the living of life, there is a continual motion of energy. In much of Gaia's life force on planet Earth, that motion is dictated by surroundings and natural events and occurrences. Animals are driven to migrate based on seasonal changes. Drought causes population decreases in herds of beasts. Abundant sun shine and rain fall create opportunity for lush growth of plants, and thus smaller creatures who rely on such an environment also flourish. In each of these examples, you can see how there is a strict cause and effect to the cycling of life. There is another way to affect life energy, and it is the path of the human.

Most creatures on Earth adapt to changing nature. You, as a member of the family human, are different. You have opportunity and cause to direct your course, and nature often is left to adapt to your actions. For a great deal of recorded history, this influence on Earth has been minimal. In recent centuries, it has grown more and more significant.

Think of this in terms of a river. The water flows naturally within its banks, rising and falling with seasonal rains. When the snow melts, rivers move swiftly. When the heat of summer rises, water evaporates and the river takes a leisurely pace. In both cases, life within adapts and continues a natural progression. In times past, humans swam or forded a river. They created canoes or other small vessels to travel on the river. Paddles and sails allowed them to move against the flow, but this did not significantly affect the nature of the river.

As humanity developed technologies that relied on fuels, smoke and soot from fires could have made some small changes in the nature of the river, but these were still relatively natural processes. The speed of the vessel might have caused a larger wake, but the river remained essentially unchanged and life within it continued with little repercussions. As fuels developed and the remnant and waste increased, the river was altered by chemicals not intrinsic to its movement and energy. As humanity developed further, the very existence of the river powered the villages and towns. The river also became the easy receptacle for waste.

The Current of Space-Time

As a human, you are moving through a stream of energy that, in a way, is comparable to a river. There is a flow to the time and space you exist within, a natural current that is contained by gravitic channeling. Other beings on the planet do not have a strong effect on this flow or are even aware of the passing of this energy. They are one with the realm of gravity in this way. They are bound to the earth.

As a human, you can become increasingly aware of the passage of this energy of space-time. Those seeking higher vibrational awareness find that their understanding of the nature of this flow increases daily. As you move within this energy, you have a choice in how you affect it. Will you maintain a clean flow? Or will you pollute the stream of time and space?

How can a human pollute this flow of energy? It is already heavy with violent emotion and oppression of recent centuries. However, like a true river, much of this can be filtered away with time. Actions on behalf of humanity can aid the purification of the river as well. Removing large amounts of debris, consciously filtering particles that stifle aquatic life forms, and actively opening tributaries clogged with ancient residue all contribute to returning clarity to the waters and thus improve the flow and cycle of life.

We ask whether you are polluting the current of space-time. You likely have in some small ways. Without realizing the effect you were creating, you may have engaged in supporting activities that were not based on principles of conscious living. It is a rare member of the family human who was raised in a high vibrational existence. That is changing, but for those of you in adulthood now, you must still make conscious choices regarding your influence on not just the space of Earth but also the flow of time.

Examine your thoughts and emotions. Are you active in the removal of heavy, unnatural belief systems from your life? Do you pay attention to the small thoughts and words that arise and are released from your consciousness and speech? Does what you say add to peace or sustain division? Do you speak healthy thoughts or only worthless platitudes? Are you open to new ways of thinking that are more natural and pure than habitual ideologies that continue only because of tradition?

To some, these words may sound like scolding or firm counsel. Those of strong spiritual energy are likely already in a practice of continual self-examination. View these words as further encouragement to continue that course. This era will be long recalled as one of difficult change. Those of you who enacted this change are strong beings. For many on Earth, the awareness of the passage of space-time is causing them stress regarding their mortality in relation to the planet. We ask that you stay strong and increase your strengths as your lives in the present incarnation conclude.

A brief examination of recorded history, even the past three centuries, will reveal that the present is among the most pleasant times that the family human has ever experienced. Allow yourself to appreciate this fact. The cleanliness of water, the availability of food, the widening access to knowledge, and the swift gains in understanding the universe around you — from the smallest particle to the largest clusters of stars — all these things created a cradle for you to grow and mature into the beings you are today.

The Flow of Life

You are the cusp of the future. The coming generation that you influenced, whether they are your own offspring or simply children you affect in passing, is altered permanently. They cannot return to the past. The generations that are born from them will put a great distance between the old ways and the new age.

Your passing through the stream of space and time is leaving things purer. Humanity in recent centuries left a rough wake in the flowing current and much by way of debris and hazards to navigate. The flow of time will purify, but your continued consciousness and attention to the space around you will hasten the process and benefit the future.

We remind you now that this is not simply a karmic exercise to balance past actions. What happens in the future will have a direct effect on your energy as it cycles back into physical existence. Do not become overly concerned with the passing away of ancient thought. Contribute new thinking to the future. It is not merely adjusting your thoughts but also speaking in a new and effective manner. This takes practice and discipline. This is where we see you, the generation that is mature today, now. You have learned how to communicate; now create conscious communications with one another. Set the example; do not follow. Listen to one another without judgment or the need to respond.

The concepts that you desire, that we in the spiritual realm share with you, are available to you. Many of you are practiced in bringing such qualities to your lives. We ask that you follow our example now. Speak your truths and desires. Speak without need for followers or disciples. The principles we advocate are simple. Be joyful. Remain peaceful. Act in love. Say these words to one another, for they create a powerful filter. In this way, the future times become pure and we experience a space where all can flourish.

CHAPTER THIRTEEN

Sense the Future

As above, so below. You exist at a turning point for humanity. More than that, you are the catalyst for a sweeping change in the vibration of planet Earth. The family human is an important factor, a vital element in the balancing of energy in the universe. You are a conscious aspect of the energy of Source choosing a fresh direction for the future.

Much has occurred in the past 300 years. We often point out this space of time to you. We also say that the next 100 years will bring amazing alterations to the way the family human conducts life on the planet. At this moment, you can clearly see the delineation between what was and what will be.

Peace Is an Active Term

The details are yet to be decided. Future generations have more to do with this than those who are currently at a mature point in life. Yet those of you at that point are still vital in securing the course of enlightened change the planetary society is experiencing.

Look carefully at the new waves of energy flowing about the global community. Can you recognize the rise of vibration in all areas of the world? In the past, violent action was often necessary for people to achieve rights and equality. Revolutions were started by those who felt downtrodden. Today the opposite is often true: We can see that violence stems first from those trying to defend the status quo.

The masses of beings who seek change now are often peace oriented. We remind you that peace is not the same as passive. Peace is an active term. It is something that you strive for. Observe the crowds in the streets protesting, seeking changes in their governments and a balancing of energy. In the past, this would have been a balancing of power. In some ways, people are not beyond that concept, but as time continues, the goal of gaining great power will fade. You can already see what will replace this.

More beings are seeking to exercise responsibility for their lives. The pursuit of a path of service to a communal section of humanity is once again considered to be noble and attainable. Having power and control over others is increasingly seen as infertile because it does not contribute to growth and prosperity. Love of others is a better path than love of power.

Many desire more fulfilling lives. A secure home coupled with physically and emotionally rewarding activity is seen as a higher goal than the mere acquisition of wealth. In and of itself, wealth is not something that one should avoid while seeking spiritual life. However, a higher vibrational approach to life will result in less of a need for material goods.

The technology of the world is liberating you from the need to carry great amounts of possessions with you. The advent of wireless communication and the expansion of this technology into entertainment, music, and visual arts are changing the mobility of society. You can freely travel the world with access to all your personal data, records, books, and music. Soon this will become easier still. We have said, "Think wireless." This aspect of technology is an intuitive one. It is an echo of what once was. We have long said that there are lost abilities returning to the family human. Now that moment is near.

The increase of technology is an important precursor to the future, and there are far more interesting advances ahead for the family human. Can you envision an organic integration of today's communication opportunities?

The Unseen Future

You are able to ponder and imagine new technologies based on what has come before. You can even explore new applications and potentials for what exists. What you do not see is the flash of inspiration that is to come. There is a need not yet known, a concept not fully developed, that will carry the next generation forward in the quest for a higher vibrational life, an increased emphasis on spiritual living. The shift in global society will be swift and dramatic. In much the same way as engines and flight amazed those accustomed to walking or riding horses, the new technologies on the horizon will marvel you.

There will continue to be those who fear change. You see them today seeking to cling to ancient concepts, labeling them "traditional" or "moral," but proving their philosophies are false by their own hateful speech and acts.

This is the ending of strong waves of old, unbalanced ways. Fear is not coming to an end, but the power of those who promote it is diminishing.

The response you see today, that of increased community and communication, is pressing the last dregs of that power away. More are interested in coming together and in learning about one another than in supporting old, outdated boundaries. Do you desire to regain freedom to travel and explore the world and to meet and engage with others? This is key to the new inspiration. This idea is approaching from a source that will not surprise everyone, but the reality will be vastly different from what is currently believed. Here too the family human will find a need to release old beliefs, but this will be eagerly and joyfully accomplished when you see the truth of life in the universe.

Enter the New World

You will need to do little to reach this moment. Like the seasons or the tide, it cannot be halted. Your continued lives and the lives of future generations are going to be altered, yet much will be the same. You will still be humans. You will still exist in the realm of gravity. You will still be subject to aging and the passing of time. This might dismay those who have attained greater years. It is true that many alive now will not see the full result of their efforts to raise the vibration of Gaia. Do not despair. Passing from the planet does not exclude you from benefiting from these changes; it simply alters your perspective.

While still on the planet, you can do much to prepare for and observe the way that things are developing. First, continue your spiritual practice. No one on Earth has achieved a state where they can cease acting in a spiritual way. Maintain your mindfulness through meditation or prayer. Remain on a path of physical wellness by focusing not on what ailments you may feel but rather on what makes you feel vital. Persist in creating a single point of awareness that consists of your healthy body, your full mind, and your connection to your spiritual family.

Second, seek community. Share with others on all levels. Simple greetings, shared resources, and expressions of humor and encouragement all lead to a strong connection among you and others. This does not mean that you must always be in agreement on topics of the day. In fact, it is good and proper to share with those who are not of like mind as well as those who are. This fully opens communication, and communication is the doorway to the new society.

Third, create images for yourself of a balanced and happy world. Integrate your own image into this, and act as if it is already a reality. For many, this will be a difficult exercise. Should you pay too much attention to fear-based reports from media outlets, you might find that you are often discouraged, that is, taken away from your heart and thus your heart's desire. By creating images of peace and prosperity, you will become aware of the many encouraging events taking place locally and globally. This will engage the heart's energy in a passage of freedom. Imagination is a far more powerful energy than people have realized. The centuries-long attempt to quell the imaginations of the populace is concluded. By creating these images, you create your own perfect life.

Fourth, recall consistently what true spiritual attributes are. By keeping the qualities of love, joy, and peace close in mind, you will find yourself at the center of a ripple of energy that changes those around you. It may take time at first, but consider yourself to be a source of these strong actions. Radiate the sense of peace you desire for the global community. Be openly joyous at the simple beauties you observe in other beings. Be bold in speaking of the strength of love, free from all bonds of the past. Love knows no rule or law. Love is.

Earth is responding to the changes of the past half century. We tell you that the struggle is not at an end, but the conclusion is in sight. Draw deeply from your loving, spiritual nature. Emanate purity from your peaceful core karmic being. Press that joyful spiritual light ahead to the future like a beacon in the night.

CHAPTER FOURTEEN

A Great Creation Begins

As above, so below. These times have often been referred to as "end times," and this is not necessarily a mistaken view. These times are not the end of all things, however. Although there is a fear-based belief that speaks of great destruction, we tell you now that there will be a great creation. In fact, it is something that has begun, and you are now called to participate more fully in it.

Many of you have a clear vision that the societies in which the family human has existed for the past 300 years are dissolving. What once worked for humanity cannot support the new beings arriving on Earth. The strong, energetic life being born today and through the next century is pushing old ways off balance and out of the way. This is an era that may be uncomfortable for many who cling to old ways. Spiritually minded beings will recognize and embrace the new paths of life.

For some time now, we have explained that there has existed a stillness to this portion of the universe. A low tide of energy left many projects and plans without the momentum for fruition or completion. Many felt a general lack of energy in relation to life itself. We tell you now that life has begun to move forward and soon will be a swift-moving wave!

There are a great many concepts that belong exclusively to the past. These ideas and philosophies are being shaken at their root systems. The foundations of long-standing institutions are cracked and crumbling, but they are massive and in some cases quite ancient, making them difficult to remove. Many seek to shore up the old walls. These ones look to the past. It is appropriate to retain lessons learned from the past, but it makes no sense to keep the structures that made those lessons necessary. Let us all move forward. There are new lessons available that are more beneficial and rewarding.

The Misguided Concept of Good versus Evil

One of the primary philosophies that must be removed for the sake of future spiritual growth is that of an absolute good versus an ultimate evil. Although there is no such thing as good or evil in the way some institutions define them, it is one of the most deeply entrenched ideas in the world. The fact that good and evil do not exist is a difficult concept for most humans to understand, but it is a critical spiritual truth.

When people seek to promote the idea that one section of humanity is evil, they are really creating a division in an attempt to gain power over others. Those labeled as "good" then feel better about themselves. This is caused by a lack of internal validation. Those who accept these thoughts are weak in their beliefs of their own positions as aspects of the universe. A spiritual individual need never feel the pull to join with others for the sake of personal validation.

Actions that can be viewed or labeled as "evil" are easily dispersed by an application of balance to life. If unbalanced humans follow another who also faces personal imbalance, the movement gains strength. When strong enough, masses of humans can create justification for many destructive and unbalanced activities, even against other members of the family of humanity. If enough balanced beings were to reject the unbalanced actions of the one or even the few, the destructive imbalance would fade and lose power.

It is important to your balance to keep in mind that there is no true state of good or evil. There are manifestations of others' failures to balance themselves. Good and evil are perceptions.

Be aware that deeply entrenched institutions will vilify new ideas and thoughts. Maintain your balance, and look at things with true spiritual vision. Ask yourself, "Will this change affect the planet in a way that supports future balance? Or will resisting this change enable the current imbalance the family human is experiencing to continue?"

There are large issues facing you. Trust your own ability to perceive the true state of the world, and do not give your perceptions over to fear-based reactions. Do not be distracted by unimportant illusions.

Forward Motion Is the Key to Personal Balance

The energy of the present will be shifting so swiftly that it will become more difficult to achieve or maintain a state of balance than at any time in recorded human history. This is not to say that it is impossible. You hear an almost constant stream of statements that are emotionally inflammatory. You witness unprecedented demonstrations of greed and socially irresponsible behaviors. There are wide gaps between people across the surface of the planet. There is little on the physical plane to demonstrate that a new level of spirituality is near. Yet this is what many of you sense. Your ability to feel this as a certainty is one of the primary qualities that will assist you in maintaining your personal level and center. Forward motion is the key to balance.

Many seek to go backward, believing that somehow things were better. We tell you now, and you can see this easily for yourselves, that the past held many societal difficulties and problems. The solutions to many of those social problems brought you to the point of spiritual evolution that exists in the present era. You are now being asked to leave behind the barriers of the past. Do not spend time seeking to remove or destroy those walls of separation. Only move forward, all of you, all of humanity, into the future where these divisions do not exist.

Continue the forward motion, and do not seek to impede others in the great growth that the family human is experiencing. It is better to erect signposts and markers to guide one another rather than walls with gates to contain or control each other.

When many are in motion, society will have a balanced advance. You have seen this at various times in the past. Sadly, such moments rarely are studied or dramatized. Instead, conflicts such as war or conquest have been publicized far more than discoveries and learning. Bring your own attention around to these greater things. Do not forget the events of violence; also do not revel in them as if some glory could be gained from slaughter. Enough blood is shed in advance of false concepts. Accept that there are better ways to achieve balance and unity than the forced extinguishment of other cultures. The future is already better than the past. Set your sights in that direction.

Strong Words

We speak to you in a strong way. Our timing is specific. The pivotal moments of the upcoming years have begun. As often happens, the events above, in the spiritual realm, precede the events below, in the physical realm. Between these two realms exist the dual realms of human emotion and thought.

It is in your emotional core that you will begin to sense the changes. It will feel like chaos at first. Much will be sensed as destruction if you are unprepared. Adjust your perceptions, and you will begin to witness opportunities for personal growth during the coming days and years. Use the information you gain to look forward. Leave behind the perceptions placed on you in the past. It is in the future that you will exist. You and all of your descendants desire a peaceful existence. Speak and see it as if it has already happened.

Do not waste your words in futile attempts to sway others from old beliefs. Your forward actions will prove that the archaic ways are weak and of little use. Ask yourself why you believe what you do, and be willing to release concretized concepts that weigh you down and hold you back. The future will be lighter in many ways.

Accept responsibility for your actions and your life. Act on your own behalf. This applies to all realms of existence: physical, mental, emotional, and especially spiritual. Take back the responsibility for your spiritual growth. Far too many have given that over to priests or gurus. Too many have abdicated their potential for communication with those of us in the realm of spirit. We are here. We are waiting to hear from you directly, not just in the sense of prayers and requests for material aid but in the true sense of relationship and sharing. We seek to converse with you. We can learn from you as much as you can learn from us! Do you believe you have something important to share? We await your input!

We always open with the phrase "As above, so below," and this is a profound concept. It has much more validity than the idea of good and evil. There is a higher level of existence that we are all being pulled toward. Even those in the realm of spirit are able to raise their vibration. Understand this: It is a cooperative effort. The closer together we are, the more harmonious our view of the future is and the faster the vibration can rise in this sector of the galaxy.

Those existing in the realm of spirit love you and all on Earth. We cannot do anything but express love, for our vibration is beyond the divisive energies that now fade from the planet. As you bring yourselves into this way of thinking, your emotions will cleanse, and peace will flow in a natural way. Begin now, in small ways if necessary, to immediately commit to moving forward and leaving the past behind. The sudden flush of joy that you experience will give momentum to your new action. Do not be sad should you lose momentum. Begin again and again until you are a natural being of love, joy, and peace.

We are here. You are not alone, and soon we will be closer still.

CHAPTER FIFTEEN

Children of the Sun

As above, so below. A shift in vibration is occurring. The vision you once perceived for the world is being altered in profound and significant ways. This is not happening easily. In a troubled world, it can be difficult for even the most spiritually minded beings to coexist. When surrounded by elements of discord, it is hard to make your own voice heard, even to yourself. It is harder still to gain a clear view of what is true and meaningful. Doing both takes great effort or a new set of eyes.

The Example of Children

Many of the children born these days are a variant of humanity. They do not respond well to having their play interrupted, and there is a difference in how they play. The topics are more serious and mature. Their imaginings are a way of looking at how life actually is and seeking ways to alter and improve it. They do not blindly accept preconceived notions or traditions. They appear to have a new light in their eyes; they see further than previous generations into both the future and the past.

Looking into the eyes of a newborn today, you might feel that they are happy to see you. It is as if they possess a clear remembrance of what has gone before. Many infants seek to speak and communicate much sooner than traditional knowledge indicates.

Comprehension of complex ideas and tools comes at a very young age and sometimes even precedes full speech abilities. Notice how many children are fascinated with cell phones and computers before they are aware of how these machines function. Perhaps you know of a child who has shown early interest in a musical instrument. What was once called prodigy will soon be called normal. We have termed this coming generation the children of the Sun.

The Harmony of Children

A harmonious life is a peaceful life. To exist in harmony does not mean that you are the same as everyone else. In music and art, harmony is a unique sequencing of notes, colors, or other forms of vibration that cooperates with and enhances other such vibrations. An infinite variety of combinations are available. As a unique being, your experiences on the planet can be brought together with the experiences of other beings, giving a new perspective on the story of life.

Children naturally sing songs and play together, creating small worlds for themselves. Their guidelines are based on enjoyment of life. Allowed to play together on their own, most children develop a natural harmonious relationship with one another. Harmony can be disrupted. Think of a song or piece of music. A discordant action from one of the participants is immediately obvious to those singing or playing along. There are many ways for a child's natural harmony to be disrupted today. It is not simply an exterior noise, but any type of invasive vibration that will separate the concord that children of today require. Consider the examples of poor nutrition or the input of disquieting concepts on a child. Also, loud or harsh noises from outside a circle of playing children can create a potential for disharmony. The tighter the group, the less likely a disruption will occur from outside.

Often children will cease their activities only when brought out of them by an authority's insistence that they alter course. Children, and indeed most other beings on the planet, learn early on that they must follow the authoritarian voice or deal with some less-than-pleasant consequence. Generally, the authority is not mistaken in redirecting the child's energy, but from the perspective of the child, it may seem as if something valuable is being taken away. The authority may have a higher perspective of what needs to be accomplished. The best parenting occurs when the child feels cooperative without being coerced or threatened by adverse action or punishments. They are conditioned to live within preset guidelines passed on from generation to generation. In many cases, however, such guidelines are based on old ways or environments and may not have validity in the new age.

Children do not naturally feel these restrictive ways. They do not demarcate their lives. They sleep when tired, eat when hungry, and play whenever possible. Is this not the exact way you would describe your ideal life? There is much to be learned from children. They do not choose companion beings based on age or gender or race. Friends are those who have fun with them when they are together. Together they accept the challenge to learn about one another, discovering the core of their own beings as well as that of others. This arriving generation is well up to the challenges they face. The best thing that can be done for them is to stabilize their physical environment, in the home or educational spaces, and allow them to rediscover principles and apply them in new and dramatically imaginative ways. Stabilizing their environment is an easier task than it might first appear. The children of the Sun already have a clear vision of what they want the world to be like.

Children Past and Present

In the more distant past, children were often raised with strong examples of sufficiency and understood the natural cycles of procreation, birth, life, and death. They were not shielded from knowing what occurred in life. They participated at a high level in the structure of the family and community, which were once tightly formed.

For several generations, especially those in the late nineteenth and through the twentieth centuries, children have had basic realities kept from them for the sake of maintaining traditions. A forceful movement to stabilize the societies of the world and create rigid order led to the institution of many rules that were not based on harmonious spiritual living. These rules were not oriented toward the growth of human potential. Inflexibility must be removed before any true advances in life can be made. Spirituality does not thrive under rigid conditions.

As recent generations have grown and discovered for themselves what their personal truths are, they began to develop insularity to what they were being told. The most recent generations are now developing their own world and, in a sense, a global language. They have begun to believe what is valuable to them is more important than the traditions of previous generations. The relevance of structures and institutions must be proven to the children of the Sun through their own observations. This sets them apart from previous generations who accepted what they were told. Even the past several generations that seemed to have a passion for rebellion eventually accepted the basic worldview passed down to them. They did not fully carry the same exploratory energy of the children now being conceived and born. They had much to overcome. The early inroads into the questioning of authority allowed for each successive generation to further break down barriers to growth. These barriers acted like dampeners for the rising vibrations. Harmony was difficult to fully realize.

The main barriers have now suffered collapse. The walls — in some cases, literal walls — have been removed, taken away, for the most part, by the youth of the planet. What was once considered to be protection is now seen as insulation or, worse, isolation. The new generations can now see each other for the first time in over a century. They see and communicate with each other not as strangers but as fellow beings. They are doing this in an instantaneous manner. This is how beings in the realm of spirit communicate with one another.

The Presence of Beings of Higher Perception

We in the realm of spirit look for those of you who enjoy your lives, who have fun, rather than for those who seek structure and strict expectations of deadlines and hard rules. The universe is not a place of harsh lines. It is a spectrum of vibrations. Bend with the universe, and you will find that pleasurable moments will increase in your life. Artificial rules are put in place in an effort to control others. Creating a sameness to all beings will ensure that no one will challenge an established routine or dogma. Ask yourself, "How well do children sit still for drawn-out speeches and lectures? How well do they behave when allowed to explore nature?" Which would you prefer?

The children being born today benefit greatly from their parents. There is a global energy that is casting away old restrictions. The generation currently becoming parents is holding on to the concept of games and enjoyment far longer than at any other time in history. It is true that this is not specific to this age group. As we have noted, there is no true boundary defining them. It has been a progression of generations, one fading into the next, that brings this growing energy into the planet.

Earth is preparing for a great burst of creativity and growth. The family human can only reflect this and consciously accept the opportunity to alter. You are of Earth. What the planet does directly affects your energies. As Earth shifts and spins into a fertile space, all beings in existence on the planet will feel the call to be fertile and to create.

We are not suggesting that procreation is a proper course for everyone. Certain responsibilities must be met to create the appropriate space for a child to be nurtured and nourished. Parents must attain a level of maturity for a child to begin a balanced life. We caution you that the changes approaching the planet are not easily dealt with, and complications in life will make things challenging. A new child is a great complication!

The Advent of the Children of the Sun

The children being born today are beings of higher vision. They are arriving in a world that is releasing boundaries daily. Societies shift by the minute, and these children will have the opportunity to create new ways of existence. It is they who will have the abilities to see beyond and greet those who approach from there.

They are the future. They can see past the old labels and demarcations. They see clearly that there are few boundaries that need to exist between beings. Theirs is not a concern of law but of learning. The presence on the planet of these ones is only now beginning to be felt and realized. Many came before them, scattered, and in a few groups at a time. The new vision of humanity is arriving in greater numbers. There will soon be overwhelming numbers of beings who are not concerned with separation or profiting over one another. It will be a world of play and exploration. Challenges will remain, and all will not be peaceful at once.

You may not see this reality, but it is there, just a short time in the future. Think of what was a mere one hundred years ago. Look at what has occurred. Imagine what will be as this path continues. Look to those who now lead, not from fear, but from potential. Support the beings on the planet who offer hope and acceptance.

The children of the Sun have an instinct for spirituality that will take the family human to places not yet imagined. You could not arrive there with the perceptual limits that exist on you now. Releasing old energies of domination and inequality will usher in the opportunity for continued growth of love between strangers. The presence of constant joy will bring a stability based on human potential rather than on conquest or possessions. The light of remembrance of spiritual existence will cast a glow of peace that is easily approached and followed.

CHAPTER SIXTEEN

Observe Changes in the Family Human

As above, so below. It is said that the only constant is change. We tell you that the best way to cope with change is to be a part of the process. For a century, there has been a concerted effort to create a society where things essentially remain the same from one generation to the next. This attempt to stop change has only served to focus the energy during one of the largest shifts of perception in recorded history. The pressure is now rapidly eroding long-standing beliefs and traditions, in some cases sweeping them away with the rapidity and intensity of a river that bursts through a dam.

How can you be a part of this process? Is it necessary to be active in violent protest or bitter arguments? Should you seek to promote a worldview? Is there a perceived wrong you should take as a cause and devote your energies toward? Let us examine the nature of the changing energy encompassing the planet.

Generational Energy

You can see that there are many things altering and shifting throughout Earth these days. It can be difficult to navigate this rapid season of change. A large part of this difficulty comes from within, for your own personal energies are also rapidly shifting. It is a rare time.

Imagine you are traveling on a river that flows north to south during the winter. You will first experience cold and possibly icy conditions. If you are drifting with the water's flow, you will be taken south, but only at the pace of the stream itself. To prevent damage to your vessel, you may need to press against ice floating down the river alongside of you. In those first days, you probably will need protective clothing and a source of heat. Soon, however, you will find that during the day you will feel less need for warm clothing. In time, any ice that may have impeded navigation will vanish, and the evening temperatures will rise. Eventually you come to a warm area, a very different climate from the one where you began your journey. It is the same river, but environmental conditions have changed.

It is much the same as you travel through the space-time continuum while existing on the planet Earth. There are climates throughout the universe, varying energies that create different levels of potential. As the solar system moves, there are continued interactions and subsequent reactions. You on Earth are subject to these occurrences, but they are vast energetic actions that take decades, centuries, or even millennia when observed from your perspective as an individual consciousness.

These shifts bring changes on levels that you have yet to measure. The quantification of such a thing has yet to be of any real interest to humanity. This was not always the case. Humans, those who have left little record of their existence, once observed these things in a powerful way. The skies were clear, and at night, it was possible for them to sense the greater nature of the universe and their space and purpose in it. You are now in an area of great fluctuations and interactions. The planet Earth and all things on it are acting and being acted on as you traverse this section of the universe. Change is not simply constant; it is intensified.

Types of Change

There are two distinct types of change that can be observed clearly in human society. The easiest, and sometimes most troubling, is physical change. The second and subtlest is spiritual change. What links these within you is the emotional and logical perception of life and your place in history.

The first type of change is subject to gravity and thus takes time, often centuries. Physical changes are obvious when they are vast. Intensive earthquakes and storms are easily observed. In these instances, there is little to do but be prepared. The climatologically based alterations to the earth are far deeper than realized or acknowledged. These have occurred before, though not in such a focused way. It is always good to increase respect for Gaia's life force. Also attributable to the energy of physical change are violent actions, whether in a revolutionary sense against a government or institution or as one lone human attacking a small section of society.

You can see the need for changes in oppressive governments or religions but might wonder at the necessity for suffering by many. This is a karmic echo of the past three centuries. It is difficult to describe to someone who has a secular vision of life. For the spiritually aware, a moment's pondering on this fact will bring a higher vision of why such violence occurs, especially in areas that have endured such behaviors throughout history.

There is no need to take part in such conflict. In fact, there is no need to exist in conflict at all. Act in an appropriate way toward the earth and Gaia, and remain peaceful with all beings when possible. In this way, you contribute to the centering and balance that will be a part of the change that is taking place. This can often be a difficult stance to take.

Soon you will see a smoother approach to large changes. Leaders in ancient religions will stand higher and release long-held biases and inequities. Their followers may still adhere to beliefs that no longer serve the future of the family human, but they will be freer to act in the energy of love and acceptance than in all of history. When these adjustments in attitude are in place, it will be impossible to return to spiritually dark times.

The second type of change is less visible. Spiritual changes happen swiftly. To the perception of the family human, these seem instantaneous. You can, in times of great need or peril, request assistance, and it will seem to be a miraculous occurrence of deliverance. It is not such an instant reaction from the perception of the realm of spirit. Also, not every request is granted. Your spiritual companions do not exist to serve you but to guide you. That said, we do seek to assist you to a greater awareness and higher vibration.

Ultimately it is up to you — the undivided one, the individual — to reach this higher level. It has not always been so. The family human has gained a level of maturity that once again allows for self-determination on the spiritual level. Will you act in a self-determined and spiritually motivated way?

The Stronger Path to the Future

Humans currently live two and sometimes three times longer than many generations of their ancestors. Because of this, a broader spectrum of human experience is available today. In addition, perception of the world has increased. The potential for higher wisdom has never been greater.

A spiritually aware being can see that higher wisdom is not common in a larger part of the population. However, you will notice a steady growth of wisdom, specifically in the youth of the world and especially in those who live in deeply troubled areas. These places, many with long histories of religious strife and repression, are also places where spiritual strength is being tested and purified. In coming decades, great spiritual leaders will appear on the world scene from places traditionally considered socially and economically backward. Wisdom will arise from unlikely countries.

Now, you must process all of these changes internally. In the greater perspective of raising vibrational existence, the individual acts as a filter for karmic energies. Here is where the emotional nature must exercise and strengthen its attachment to the spiritual vision. By doing this, you reduce the reactive energy that causes anger against perceived injustice, or what is actually imbalanced yin energy. By strengthening the logical approach to the physical changes, you create opportunity for a lessening of violent reaction by giving yang a purposeful direction of growth.

In general, there is now more of a regular flow of energy to the human experience than in recent decades. This will increase over the next few years, and already you may sense that life energy is becoming less abrupt. As we are pointing out, there is much that can be accomplished to ease the effects of such a way of life. There is still a long passage of time before Earth can return to a status of smooth flow.

A continuing emphasis on the true spiritual principles of love, joy, and peace is necessary from the perspective of the realm of spirit. It is not meant as a criticism, as if you are unaware of these basic spiritual paths. It is to nurture and strengthen you, our intent being to balance the constant pressure of emotional reaction or mental aggression that consumes so many of the family human on the planet at this time.

It is your determination that fuels the next generations. The strength of love you display will be remembered long after the events of violence. The joy you take and infuse in your life, despite bleak reports and difficult days, will be the pattern set for children now being born. The peace that you insist on, that you act on, is the counterbalance for the waves of despair that are translated into anger and recrimination. Love, joy, and peace have little concern for the past. They are energies of observable change, and they mark the path of the future.

CHAPTER SEVENTEEN

Earth in the Balance

As above, so below. Many of you see the planet Earth in very different terms from the current leadership of your societies. Many of you see humanity in very different ways from those same societies. You are troubled by what might appear to be indifference to the plight of many members of the family human and to other beings you recognize as valuable to the planet. Living today is unbalanced in many ways. It is therefore difficult to conduct your own life in a spiritual way and to successfully navigate the day-to-day physical functions necessary to create a home and haven for yourself and your family.

It is true that balance is hard to achieve, but it is not impossible. This truth calls for action on behalf of the individual. There is a greater balance waiting to be achieved, and this requires your attention now. We often say, "Balance yourself." That is a key teaching in all true spiritual instruction. Now we direct your attention outward to give you perspective.

Spirituality is ultimately the act of accepting and activating your personal energies. There is a point at which the individual, the undivided one, makes a choice to act in a balanced way, marking the beginning of a spiritual path. Next, he or she then can simply act in a balanced way without needing to question or choose a course. This is true spiritual living. It is a difficult thing to do as an individual on the planet at this time. Earth is not currently a well-balanced place, but you can assist in balancing its energies.

A time of great choice is upon you. This has been intensifying for several years, and now it has come to a specific point. There are many aspects to this choosing, and the process will continue for some years — perhaps decades — but here and now we in the realm of spirit see a clear moment.

We are not giving a prophecy. Prophecies are easily misunderstood. We are explaining the momentous time in which you exist and illustrating the path of energy as we see it playing out. Look about you, and note the choices you are being asked to make. Listen to our words, and examine them with your heart to see whether they have value in guiding your selection.

In all of history, there has never been a time like now. The balance of energies has been far out of alignment for several thousand years. The physical Earth has been affected in many ways, but the family human specifically has struggled with this imbalance. In this way, you in the physical realm and we in the spirit realm have been acting as a filter for this energy. It has taken a long time, and acting in consciousness, we have made choices that will benefit Source energy in meaningful ways. The result will be a great awakening of harmony and peace for us all. First we must move in specific ways to create a full and smooth change of direction for the energies we term yin and yang.

Support Yin

The energy of yin is rising. There will be a balancing of the two aspects of energy in the galaxy soon. For some time now, the energy of yang has been dominant, especially on planet Earth. At the same time, the energy of yin was not acting to its strength. This is altering.

Let us pause to define the terms "yin" and "yang." In many parts of the world, these are misunderstood as gender based, or female and male. The vision is not entirely in error, but it limits this energy greatly.

The actuality of yin is one of nurturing and growth, comfort and healing. Certainly we can see that the male is capable of these qualities. Yang, then, is one of structure and support as well as creative action and formation. These attributes are clearly represented in the feminine. To separate them out is to limit each gender. Yet that is precisely what many organizations — particularly religious ones but also more recently governmental structures — have been attempting to do for many centuries. This is futile. It is like trying to separate Earth from its Moon or preventing night from following day. There are natural ways that the universe operates. We delineate the nature of yin and yang to explain the basic aspects of Source.

There are those who will attempt to place one energy over another. They will also try to gain power over other beings. This is imbalanced yang acting without the presence of yin. This is yang in pain.

If yang is unbalanced, then yin will be as well. But as we stated earlier, this is in the process of change. How can you as an undivided one who is acting in a spiritual way affect this process? You can activate and exercise your yin energies to make them stronger. Consciously make intuitive choices. Sharpen your intuition. Avoid subjecting your feelings to the structure of logic too early in your attempts at creating a fulfilling, balanced life. Be aware that, at first, you might be yielding to personal desire and creating wish-fulfillment fantasies. These are not necessarily choices with little value. Some who may be in a weakened yin condition might give in to fear-based intuition and sense danger. Be aware that what you sense could be a challenge to your own preconceived notions.

Practice yin. You will find that your levels of physical strength will respond slowly and your emotional levels of strength will be challenged. You will also experience a heightened awareness of spiritual connection. Draw your power from this, and then allow yang energies to assist in structuring your visions.

See Past False Images

By increasing your yin energies, you will comprehend the true motivations of others. In strengthening your personal yin, follow these brief guidelines: Do not take people at face value. Do not believe everything you hear others say. There are many looking to continue to profit from dominance and fear. They will appeal to your fear and offer you empty images. They can only succeed if you give in to their desires. Yin is peaceable but is not submissive.

Understand that avoiding conflict is not necessarily a balanced spiritual approach. The resolution of conflict in a peaceful way is spiritual, and this is a primary aspect of the purpose of Earth as a filter. Yin is the only way to truly peaceful living. No strong yin-based society will engage in warlike behavior. Strong yin will resolve conflicts without sending the young off to perish for the interests of others.

Support Women and Children

This is perhaps the easiest thing to observe and use as an indicator of the true motivation behind certain religious and political movements: What is the position taken on behalf of women? Are they considered an equal force, or are they treated as subservient to males? Is there an opportunity for full participation, or are they relegated to minor service duties? Are women viewed as property to be owned and controlled, or is there an opportunity for the wisdom of yin to shine through and strengthen society?

Children carry a naturally balanced yin and yang energy. When observing movements and causes, ask yourself, "Are children being encouraged to express themselves fully, or are they being suppressed and taught that they are, at their basic nature, wrong or evil? Is there an attempt to control what the children learn, limiting access to basic knowledge about life, or is there a pure and honest approach to nature and the natural way of life on the planet?"

Understand that even though a woman or child might be involved in a prominent way within a movement that involvement is not proof of balanced or strong yin energy. Symbols are not reality.

Do not detract from yang energy. Yin will direct yang and give it purpose. Yang exists to provide support and structure. It is not a dominating force unless it senses that there is no clear path available and action is required. This is why yin's direction is vital.

The creation of a peaceful, harmonious life for all beings on the planet is within sight. We have been near this before, yet it remains to be achieved. A push of yin energy by many beings can tilt the direction of the energy of the family human. Without strong yin direction, it is possible that we will experience a longer time of yang imbalance. We seek to activate your yin strengths now with these words.

Seek to love everyone. This is not to say that imbalanced yang is to be tolerated; rather, do not react to imbalanced yang with unbalanced yin. Expressing love to everyone is a difficult thing. When encountering a challenging person, simply say to yourself, "I love this one and his or her true balanced nature." The effect on that person will be deep in an energetic way.

Create moments of joy for those who are in a weakened condition. This can be achieved in many creative ways, but remain alert to the necessities of life that such people have. Share what you have. Care for those who have needs. Say to yourself, "I enjoy bringing joy to others." The effect on you will be deep in an energetic way.

Nurture peace. Seek moments when peace is natural, and invite others to enter that space and time. Join in peaceful pursuits. Act in peacekeeping efforts. Say to yourself, "I am at peace with everything and everyone." The effect on the planet will be deep in an energetic way.

CHAPTER EIGHTEEN

Take Action for Future Harmony

As above, so below. We have said that a new way of life is approaching. We have said that the future holds a higher vibrational form of living. We tell you now that this process has begun. Many of the old blocks of energy are being transformed into new paths of motion. The low tide of energy that you have existed in for more than a decade is now beginning to rise. Already many of you sense this shift. You feel the energy being released back into your lives. You are witnessing motion in areas of your lives that you thought were solid and stuck.

This motion is just a small indication of the wave of change that you will experience in the coming decades. It is time now for everyone who is striving for spiritual awareness to fully engage his or her senses. Look intently at the approaching days and the choices you are making. Step into the beings that you wish to become with strong intention and firm image. Create a meaning to existence that is dramatically different from the strife and fear that has been fostered in the past several thousand years.

Now is the time for all beings to act in accord with their deepest desires for peace. Those on the planet today are setting a unique course for future generations to have a deeper life of great meaning. Life has meaning, but you must create that meaning for yourself.

Strength amid Pressure

Changing times demand strength. There is still much weight from the past that will continue to exist. An important aspect of the shift is that action must be taken to dislodge the remainder of old thought and outmoded philosophies. The effort necessary will be made easier by the flow of energy available in the present. There will be a natural motion of erosion that will allow for the shifting of concepts. This does not mean all will be attained with ease. There will continue to be a pressure on all beings.

The strength that you must exert will, in part, cause that pressure on you. You are pressing against weighty things. We caution you not to lose your balance or peace in this activity. It is not a battle you are engaged in; you are simply moving something heavy out of the way. You do this on behalf of future generations.

The thought of more pressure being put into life is almost unendurable for many. The idea that the near future will be less stressful does not carry the comfort that it once did. You are at the tipping point, the moment of critical mass, when decision and action cannot be recalled. The energy around the planet is very intense. Rest when you need to. Know that we in the realm of spirit have been working in this same manner for some time now. We will continue. It is now the time for those of you incarnate on the planet to engage your efforts as well.

We do not tell you this to bring fear or to enforce an ancient belief in mythic punishment and reward. We say these words now to help you gain a higher vision, a perspective that many living on Earth either cannot or refuse to accept. These days are not end times. They are part of a continuum of time. If you must place a marker along the timeline, you can consider it a time of renewal. If you compare this time in history to the changing seasons, we have entered into a robust spring, one that is following a hard winter.

Some ways through these times are easier than others. Some people will choose to struggle through, looking backward and wishing that they could return to the past. Their progress will be painful. They will only see things diminish. We tell you now to look upward and forward, and you will witness amazing things beginning to arrive.

The state of individual empowerment is growing, and it is now unstoppable. The family human has arrived at a point of maturity. All who incarnate on Earth will be prepared to accept greater responsibility for their lives than any generation has since before recorded history. You see this in many disparate ways. Soon, many things will begin to come together. There will be concerns about privacy and freedom of thought. Do not despair. New technologies will not deter the movement toward full freedom of choice. They will create a level society that allows for increased equality, but it will take some time. Many will fight against this equalizing. We have said before and we remind you now that the next one hundred years will see a great change in society. This will mark a point of evolutionary growth for the planet itself. The family human will be affected in many wonderful and fulfilling ways. The Harmonic Coalescence is in effect, and this energy is growing. Many aspects of life are being altered and will continue to come together.

Initiate Peaceful Action

You have lived through much in the way of intensified times. The energy around the planet is wound like a coil, and the release seems imminent to many. There is a choice to be made, and the family human has much to do with this choosing. Will the release of energy be a thing of peace, or will it become an action that must force away all old restrictive thought and habit?

We have spoken of the past three centuries as a time of great variance, and you can see the result of this rapid action. Advances in many fields give testimony to the great power of the human mind. Many tragic internecine wars and religious oppressions give evidence of the imbalance the planet has experienced. Balance is returning. Will you be a balancing energy, or will you choose to cast support toward things that are contentious?

The stress that has built up will be released. It can occur in one long, smooth release or as a sharp, sudden crack. Consider the example of sound waves. There can be one long, controlled note that others can harmonize with, or there can be a cacophony of shouting with each voice trying to drown out the others. Which is more pleasant? Which do you hear now? Which are you personally engaged in?

Actions need to be initiated. You cannot rely on intervention from elsewhere. Passively waiting for someone else to take action on your behalf is a sign that your yin energies are in an imbalanced state.

The old, heavy energies that must and will be transformed are not physical in nature, though there are physical results from their existence. These old energies are beliefs and philosophies. We have spoken of these things for many years now. Become aware of them anew.

Any concept that takes away power from women or children is an old, unbalanced concept. Any philosophy that supports antagonistic conflict is a contradiction to the basic laws of the universe. The idea that one human could have an exclusive connection to a god or goddess is a falsehood. Any principle that dictates one race, one gender, or one nationality is somehow inherently better than another is patently misguided and ultimately weak. Each of these examples steers people away from their true spiritual nature.

Each of these examples is a display of imbalanced yang dominating unbalanced and weakened yin.

Support yin energy through the action of supporting women and children. This is performed through the action of love.

Cease existing in an antagonistic way. This may be very difficult in these days of tightly wound energies. When you are feeling anger or fear, ask yourself deep questions. Prepare to release old stories and histories. Act in peaceful ways. Cease acting against things. Cooperate with the natural movement of the planet and the life on it, and you will see with a clear spiritual sight what must be assisted to move and change.

Embrace your individual connection to the realm of spirit. You have no need for intercession. You are a spiritual being engaged in a physical cycle of existence; all members of the family human are. None is superior to another. All are experiencing Source energy in a unique way. Take joy in this experience, and strengthen one another when acting in the course of love or creativity.

The state of the world is altering in visible ways. The changes are sweeping. It may not always look like progress to you, but do not despair. Many beings are finding their voices in these times of transition. They need practice to sing their songs in a pure and harmonious way. Have you been practicing your song? Are you speaking and acting in ways that create harmony?

CHAPTER NINETEEN

An End to Global Conflicts

As above, so below. Often we speak of a better world, one of harmony and peace. We say to you now that this is a truth that cannot be prevented. Much must occur before this eventuality. There are conflicts approaching. Do not be afraid of these words! They are to guide you. Conflict does not always mean violence. Within the approaching conflicts will be a lessening of violence on the planet. Violence will not resolve these conflicting ideologies. Already you can see that there is more communication of individual beings on Earth than at any time in the history of the planet. Soon this will lead to a global evolution.

Guide Your Personal Evolution

It is not possible for one species to evolve alone. All life is in a constant state of adaptation. Even in the realm of spirit, there is evolution. In the physical sense, much time passes as these changes settle in and become solidified. In the spiritual sense, the adaptations can occur in what seems like an instant to those in gravity.

There are methods that will speed the spiritual evolution of physical beings. Education is required. You must retrain your brains to perceive life on Earth differently. So much of the new energy that now is flowing through the solar system is based on change and alters the way life is lived. There is so much more power available to all beings. The results of exercising this personal power will be to extend all life, expand perception, and strip away illusions no longer necessary to the growth of Gaia's children.

For far too long, you have been schooled in ways that structured your lives to fit a certain pattern. In many ways, that pattern suited a majority of the members of the family human. The stabilizing effect allowed for rapid growth of technologies and the categorization of information. However, this structuring also created limits to behavior and belief. Much of what you know is merely opinion repeated.

Be Healthy and Vital

You have been instructed that life has a certain limitation and that, as you age, there is an inevitable deterioration of your physical form. Part of that is truth but not to the extent that is widely believed. There is a new way of envisioning life. You are aware of some of these new views. Many of the concepts of the foods that are healthy and promote growth have altered dramatically in the past several decades. The detrimental effects of medications are becoming more widely known. The rampant use of prescribed drugs is on the edge of a revolution. Soon you are likely to witness a prolonged conflict regarding the use of dietary supplements versus medications.

What can you, as a spiritually minded being, do to create a higher-vibrational awareness in this matter? All evolution begins with an individual adapting to a new environment. The adaptation then is passed along to others. Physically, this is achieved through genetics and the rearing of offspring. Socially, this is brought about through discourse and the sharing of ideas. The most effective social movements begin to form organically, not organizationally.

In caring for your health, it is essential to practice a vitality-based lifestyle, one focused on increasing your health rather than treating individual symptoms through a recovery-oriented philosophy. As a recovery-oriented person, you will constantly be looking at past dis-ease in your physical form. You will be searching to prevent some illness from recurring. This is a type of fear.

Instead, look to the future and choose a different course, one focused not on past events but on future desires. Decide that movement and proper nutrition is a priority, and then begin to act on that decision. Assume that you are already healthy, and the energy will begin to arrive to help you shift your lifestyle.

Pay attention. Use your powerful brain to become knowledgeable about true health and vitality. This alteration will not occur instantly. Remember, you are within the gravity well and thus are subject to time. Here is the possibility to speed up your personal evolution. Once the thought is in place, the body can begin to respond. Even if you do not have great success at first, remember that this is a process.

Often we say, "Begin with the heart." The heart often desires ease and comfort and does not naturally set a course of discipline for the body. The brain, on the other hand, is very concerned with the physical state of life.

By taking personal responsibility, you create a single point where energy can gather. You will find others of a similar vibrational quality, and then more will find you. In this way, the world begins to shift. If you are paying attention, you will know that it already has started!

A Shift of Power

Another point of conflict will come in the form of dominion, or power shifts. You will see this happening in many places across the world. Soon it will be a stronger movement within all society. For thousands of years, a small class of humans has accepted responsibility and ruled over many. In recent centuries, there has been a clear motion that indicates a growing maturity of the family human. Like a growing child, there has been a desire for personal liberty and choice.

You have been schooled to believe that liberty and freedom exist in certain regions. To an extent, this is true. We tell you now that there will be a far greater freedom available in the very near future. No longer will you be subject to the rigid traditions that have held so many in thrall.

Again, it is the brain that must be used first. There is a sense of logic growing among the newer members of the family human. Some must first reject all things that are called spiritual. What they are really rejecting are dogmatic religious beliefs designed to provoke fear in an attempt to control others. These no longer have a place in the rising global society. When logic is applied to the many ancient superstitions that have been promoted as truth, it clearly shows that these traditions no longer promote integrity. In fact, many of these traditions symbolize a lack of integrity.

Spirituality will continue to experience a growth, however. True spirituality recognizes higher values and deeper core energies of the family human. Do you feel these deep energies? Ask yourself, "What do I feed my mind? What do I allow into my brain? What values do I place within my consciousness?"

For the time being, leaders are necessary and, generally speaking, beneficial. The humans who seek leadership are becoming clearly delineated. There are those who pursue a cause of maintaining old thought. They emphasize so-called traditional values. They speak of being ruled by written guidance that was given to societies that no longer exist. Their rule books and knowledge are not part of the current energy that is flowing through the system.

There are others who speak of global forums. They speak and act in ways that support women and children throughout the world. They work for the betterment of humankind and not for the growth of large-scale organizations.

Within both groups, there are those who might act in extreme ways or become diverted from a true spiritual course. Both must acknowledge spiritual principal above religious dogma. That time is near. One group is progressive and looks to the future whereas the other seeks to return to past ways. The first group will release the dogma. The second will fade away into history.

Invent the Future

Do you fear change? Do you find yourself wishing to return to old ways? Think deeply on these matters. Look at the larger picture. Seek to comprehend the global scale of response necessary to attain the peaceful future we speak of. We in the realm of spirit are not the ones who will bring this peaceful future! It is the members of the family human living today who will do so. The course has been set by the generation now beginning to exit the planet and is being adjusted by those who have reached maturity. Their children are testing that course now and adding new information. They are creative in a capacity that few could imagine a generation ago. The children yet to be born have a potential that cannot be imagined by those alive today except in the strongest of dreams.

To achieve higher levels of health and vitality and to gain the greater individual freedom that is approaching, you must more fully engage your brain. You will need to hone your thinking processes to a higher degree than you currently enjoy. Press yourself to examine new facts and concepts. Open your thoughts to fresh ideas and technologies. Filter out any commentary that breeds fear about the desperate nature of the planet, and witness the beauty and strength of all the beings in existence.

Understand that Earth, Gaia herself, is once again in a state of evolution. She will alter and you will adapt, just as you always have. Logic will tell you that the spiritual concepts of love and joy and peace will assist you as survival mechanisms, not just for your personal life and the lives of your generation, but truly for all generations in the future.

Love has created this opportunity to exist as a physical being aware of your spiritual nature. Joy of the knowledge of life feeds that love. Peace is the harvest, gathered when you feed your thoughts on love and joy. Focus your strong brain on these thoughts, and witness the process of evolution within your own physical form.

CHAPTER TWENTY

The End of Ancient Prophecies

As above, so below. It is now a time of passage. We have seen three elements of change — the Harmonic Convergence, the Harmonic Concordance, and the Harmonic Coalescence — occur in fewer than fifty years. This compression is rare throughout the universe. Generally, when such dramatic alterations of energy flow happen, a great destructive force is released. On the planet Earth, many of you heard the words of those who felt they could see the future. They were not completely in error, but you can now see the way that potentially catastrophic destruction has been spread out and softened. This is due in large part to the actions of a few beings on the planet. They are few, but their numbers are growing. Are you one of these beings? Would you like to be?

Misuse of the Gift of Prophecy in the Past

The future is changeable. Many decisions made in the present can have great impact on the direction of humanity's future. It is not wise to peer too far ahead nor a worthy pursuit to attempt to envision exact events. You likely will be mistaken in your perception.

Sometimes beings can gain access to a flow of time that allows for sight further along its spiral. Be cautious if this happens to you. Your perception will shift and change many times before you arrive in gravity at the moment that you perceived. This does not mean that these insights are without value. Let us speak of the prophets of old. They clearly witnessed something monumental occurring in this day and age. Each came from a specific background, and so his or her interpretations were delivered with a cultural bias that is unavoidable to those who find themselves in a prophetic flow. Some of these humans sought to guide others, and some sought to gain power and influence. Here, then, is where the breakdown in value occurs.

When the information gained from a spiritual pursuit is sacrificed to a lower-vibrational activity, such as the creation of a hierarchy or political system, its value swiftly becomes so diluted as to have no worth at the vibrational level intended. In other words, spiritual teachings can become polluted by wrong intention.

Today you can see the effects clearly. Religions that proclaim peaceful intention yet act in a manner that causes death, poverty, and subjection of other beings are obviously polluted by this lower-vibrational energy of conquest. It may be that the original words of the founders of such religions still carry truth and strong spiritual messages, but the actions of those who lay claim to the founders' legacies often betray themselves in quite obvious ways. Is your own sight clear? Can you observe the things of spiritual value and separate yourself from activities that create violence and hate? If so, you are the basis for the future.

The Lost Prophecies of the Feminine

Have you noticed that the voice of the feminine is almost completely absent in these majority teachings that pass for religion? How is it that this occurs? In the ways of yin energy, the manifest power of women is as nurturers and caregivers. In the ways of yang energy, the manifest power of men is as builders and protectors. Yet this is not the way it is translated in religion. Now, it seems that in many areas of the world it actually has gotten worse. This is a concern for many of you. We tell you now that you are not alone in this concern. We in the realm of spirit are now in motion to create a balance in this regard. We seek your actions as well.

It is not that the voice of the feminine was not able to see and prophesy. It is that their interpretation was not one that the imbalanced yang was able to use to further its own ends. In the past, just prior to the recorded histories that you possess, the voice of the women was a treasured thing. The loss of that balance, due to energies that needed to be processed over time, is not a permanent thing. The time has now arrived for many of the lost prophecies to be revealed.

The vision of great destruction was in error. It was a vision of immense change that men observed, but they sought to protect a status quo and their place in power. Of course, it looked like destruction from their vantage point. In the fear of change is the seed of corruption.

What the women observed and spoke of was a time of great growth. First, though, they saw the natural order of things. There was much that needed to be overturned. The women observed it in this way, as a plow turning heavy, densely packed earth. They could see that the work required great effort on the part of the ploughman. They witnessed the group effort involved in moving large stones and trees to prepare fields that could sustain crops. They could see that people could use the wood for shelters and cooking fires and the stones for protective enclosures. They envisioned great areas of the earth changed for the good of a community.

There is more to that vision, but for now, understand that the catastrophic destruction envisioned was at best a misinterpretation. At worst, it was manipulation to gain power over others. There are some who still seek to use this erroneous interpretation of a true spiritual vision. There are some who still seek to lay claim to the term "prophet," who still seek to gain control over the world. Their lives are short. They are imbalanced. Do not be swayed from a true spiritual path at this critical time.

An Altered Future

Many have sought to place a specific date on what was once called the "Time of the End." Notice that all those dates have passed, and still Earth abides. Still humanity loves and laughs. Still you seek the pleasure of true spiritual connection.

You can see now that dates and times are not to be feared. This realization can be the beginning for a larger number of the family human to engage in a deepening connection to their spiritual companions. Many will still perceive us as guides or angels, but we remind you that we are like you and are above only in vibrational existence, not in importance.

We ask those of you who are spiritually mature beings to be more vocal about the qualities you possess. Act more openly. Cease withholding your words because you fear ridicule. Speak in ways of love.

Those who act in error are still precious beings who carry a karmic energy of great pain. Do not hate them. They are acting a part in a greater passage of energy. You are balancing greater energies than you can imagine while incarnate. Do not insist on change for these ones. Only show them a better way, a better life. Many more will respond than you might believe at this moment in the process.

Listen for new messages from beyond the realm of gravity. It is not long now before amazing communications will occur across the planet. How will you know when such a message is clear or pure? These thoughts will not be limited to one group or individual. There will be no single spokesperson. Much of the information will be transmitted by strong yin-based beings: women, children, and a few men.

There will be a moment of global awareness. The mass communications you currently possess will glow with these new thoughts and revelations. The children born in these days of passage are already reaching for this knowledge. They are prepared for advanced communications and thus communities. They are different from you and represent the final stages of the change you are living through.

The passage is nearly at the halfway point. We say this knowing that some will still seek a specific date. There is no specific date. This is not an event with a conclusion; it is an era of transformation. Now, you are here.

We ask for your actions. We in the realm of spirit wish to link our energy more closely with yours. This is a personal choice for every being on the planet. The future population will find this separation to be unusual. They will exist in this close relationship naturally. It is opening for all, but few will achieve it in the current generations.

What, then, can you do to fulfill the lost prophecies? These are simple things, and we have said them constantly since we began our written communications.

- Rejoice at the concept of life on Earth. It is a fine and beautiful world. There is much to enjoy while incarnate. Find joy in life with others wherever you travel.
- Love the life that you have. In loving your own life you will bring greater power and strength to your physical being and connect at ever-deeper levels to your emotional and mental capabilities. This will lead you to strong spiritual vision, clear and pure. In this state, no deceptions against you will be possible.
- Peacefully coexist. All beings are perceptive. All perceptions have value. All perceptions can alter and will do so more easily and swiftly when greeted in peace.

The future that was once feared is now here, and we tell you now to proceed without fear into the next stage of change. Make your passages into these times in a state of love, joy, and peace. In this way, you are creating a world of spiritual strength.

CHAPTER TWENTY-ONE

Regain Your Lost Abilities

As above, so below. In your world today, you are experiencing a wave of change, one that is not always gentle. Much is being washed away. For some, this is a difficult time. They perceive that many things of value are eroding. They see the past as something that needs to be preserved. This perception is far from the truth.

The past is a long stream of energy. What is recalled is not the larger picture but a limited view that often does not even agree with itself. The wave that is washing away the present ideologies is revealing powerful ancient ways that the family human has forgotten. Clinging to the recent past does not offer a solid foundation of safety. Those who do so risk being washed away.

Recent changes in policies throughout the world indicate that humanity is rising to what may appear to be a new level. We tell you that you have been here before, and from the perspective of the spiritual realm, now is an exciting moment. We have long said that yin energy is rising. Witness now the strength of this rebalancing. Beyond this, imagine the next level.

What is leading to this? A receding of yang is a part of the process, but we have seen yang recede in a natural fashion before, and recently. A better way to understand this is to think of efforts to soothe a crying child. You may not understand or comprehend the distress the child feels, but you try certain actions to relieve it. Is there fear? Apply a feeling of warm comfort. Are there physical needs? Adjust the environment or change the child's clothing. Is there hunger or thirst? Supply food or drink.

Yang Renewed

Imbalanced yang has been increasingly shrill in its calling out. There has been much fear incorporated in its speech and communication. It is not yet soothed. As you might do with a child, you must sometimes allow a fit to run its course and let the energy exhaust itself. If the nurturing yin presence is in a weakened state, this course of action may exhaust those energies as well. Thus, in a child's early development, it is good to have supportive family members nearby. The number of members of the family human who are of a strong yin is now increasing. Collectively, they can soothe distressed yang. Soon this strong yin will rise even higher.

Yang energy will again find purpose but not in its previous form. Gone will be the need for anger and violent action. The truth is that there has been little need for those imbalanced actions for many millennia. This is a byproduct of a necessary development in the forgotten past. It has taken this long to rebalance yin and yang because of the extreme nature of past solar events. Now, we have crossed a threshold of energy. Now, existence can and will return to past levels. The work of humanity on the planet is ready to move to a higher level of consciousness.

Reconnect with Gaia

We will give you a simple explanation of the coming steps in Gaia's growth. We say "Gaia's growth" because this is the time when increased awareness of the planet's life force will come to the forefront. In the forgotten past, all beings felt the connection they shared with the earth's vitality. That lost connection is returning strongly.

Many have long sensed what they interpret as distress within the planetary consciousness. They have sought to rescue Earth. It is not a case of saving the planet. It is a case of reconnection and reintegration. It must first be felt by the conscious beings on the planet today. This means you must, as a society, reconnect with one another across the globe. The surge of technology in communication has made reconnecting possible. Learn to use this tool wisely. It is echoing an ability from the past, an ancient skill once known to humans but lost to most who exist today. It is not that you are incapable, but that it is suppressed. You have been taught that it does not exist, yet you have created a technology that does essentially the same thing. As there were in the remembered past, there are many now who seek to control and limit this form of communication. They cannot. This results in confusion for them and then fear.

Do you sense the true nature of this lost form of communication? Have you had experiences of nonverbal communication with others at a distance?

Have you often thought it to be a true ability? Soon you will begin to hear of those who are involuntarily communicating with others without the need for proximity. They are sensitive beings, but they are also strong beings. They will learn to guide their ability through experimentation. They will have an intuition and understand that they do not need to control this ability, only hone it. Their children will be born into a new reality.

It is not only humans they will commune with. These beings will also strongly sense the needs of the planet. Individually they cannot fully assist Earth. There will be a coming together of those who possess such skills. The joining of minds, of hearts and brains, and of feelings and thoughts will grow planetwide. The artificial barriers will drop, slowly at first, and then they will be raised once again. This process will be repeated until they are only points on a map and no longer boundaries to prevent movement.

Humanity will no longer seek to control Gaia. They will acknowledge the wisdom of her patterns and adjust their own living spaces. Technologies will develop that allow the family human to remain at a high level of civilization and to become increasingly integrated into Gaia's energetic pathways. You are seeing some of these already in the advancements of wind and solar energy use. There is much more to learn. There is energy everywhere.

Production of food will become smaller in scale without losing the variety currently available. There is a crisis that looms regarding food production. This will be resolved in one of two ways. There can be a forced return to earth-based farming that uses older, natural methods, or there can be a consensual approach to the elimination of technologies that have multiple stages of consequence on future growth cycles. The better way, the way of a higher vibrational existence, is to reach that consensual path soon. You can assist in this. Become aware.

Make Time to Listen

We understand that many are aware of certain challenges that exist. We ask you to reach a different awareness. We have just described the future of humanity and the return of one lost ability. You can prepare the way now through a simple practice.

Create a place of quiet. It is possible to find quiet places, but we ask that you consciously create an area or specific moment when you and all things that you can directly influence become quiet. There may be others who are making noise. This is not about them. This is about you. You sit quietly with only your breath and the slight sounds you make as you adjust your physical form for comfort. Do not pay attention to what is outside of you. Listen to your thoughts. Begin to direct your thinking to the immediate area of Earth that you are on. Wherever you are, you can do this simple thing. Let your own thoughts quiet down. Listen without judgment or preconceived notion. Pay attention to the communication that comes from Gaia, from Earth itself. What you hear will be her patterns. She is in constant motion. Listen not to learn what you must do but to hear what she is doing. In this way, you can increase your own awareness of Gaia.

In this way too, you begin to create a larger field of consciousness. Your quiet space will become a place where inharmonious vibrations can slow and dissipate. Gaia's vibration can then rise within this space with greater ease. All of Gaia's energy is vital and creates growth. Creating this space of quiet creates a clear point for ease of growth.

This activity does not need to be done in a garden or forest although doing so will be of benefit. It is more difficult to do in the midst of a city, building, or highly populated area. Yet the most benefit will be derived from just such an action.

True Spirituality

Gaia carries her own wisdom. Now is the time for you to listen. What appears to be distress may in fact be Gaia acting on her own behalf. She senses the universe around her in ways that the family human cannot. She prepares herself for coming changes. Her communication to you is instruction for your benefit. She tells you now how best to prepare yourselves for the new age. There are lessons available for those with clear senses.

It is time for strong yin energy to be displayed by all spiritually minded people. This includes acting consciously and releasing judgment of the past. The future is the important focus now, but paying attention and gaining clarity regarding where human society is currently at is a vital step.

We often say to you: "Love, joy, and peace." These elements are the path to and the results of true spirituality. These principles are found in many philosophies, but they are often the least practiced or expressed. We offer you this reminder: Apply the feeling of love. Adjust the environment for joy. Supply the necessary energy for peace.

We bring you these words now so that you can shape the future: Apply feeling. Adjust the environment. Supply necessities.

CHAPTER TWENTY-TWO

Begin a New Age of Balance

As above, so below. We bring you a larger and stronger message. It is not meant to cause fear or conflict. We bring a perspective from a higher vibration. We offer you a greater picture of the history of the planet and the family human.

We exist in the realm of spirit while you exist in the realm of gravity. This does not make your existence less worthy. Ultimately we are you, and you are we. The future for all will be written based on the understanding of the present. Lessons from the past will assist in a clear perception of the present. Clarity of vision is vital. It is the future that you create now.

A Galactic Rebalancing of Energy

For centuries many of the family human have attempted to acquire physical matter in the form of money, possessions, and even the unusual concept of ownership of sections of the planet. All these are areas in which many members of the family human have placed their energy and focus.

The energy of acquisition is a yang force. The energy of growth is yin. All beings alive on the planet are going to experience a deep change in the energy of life. Yin is rising. After many tens of thousands of revolutions around the strong yang force you call the Sun, balance is now imminent in the solar system. This extends far beyond what is commonly known. There are more, unseen energies out and away from the orbiting planets and bodies than you are currently aware of.

Regaining yin and yang balance on Earth is part of a major energy shift occurring in this sector of the galaxy. In many ways you, while on the planet, are protected from the strongest forces in motion. As you read these words, you know that you are past the peak of this shift. You also must realize that the strong changes that occurred over the past 200 years will be mirrored by a relaxation of pressure over the next long cycle. We have said before that there is a great alteration that will occur in the coming generations. In one hundred years, the society that exists will seem magical to your perceptions. The seeds of that society exist in you today.

Much of this balancing will consist of a redistribution of energies. In the same way that a tire is balanced by applying slight weight adjustments, so too will human society begin to balance by a careful observation of who is in control of energy that will be better used elsewhere. There will be continued resistance to such a shift, but it will gain a critical mass of motion. This is not a thing that can be halted, but it is an action that can be sped up by cooperation. We commend those who are already of a cooperative mind. You are more in alignment with the rest of the universe than those who continue to seek to acquire beyond their needs. The shift is not an easy thing to accomplish on the planet at this time. We remind you that you are not alone in existence. There are others who approach your system, seeking to join with us all again.

A Global Rebalancing of Energy

One aspect of the balancing of energy here on the planet is the growing awareness of how to act in concert with Gaia. It is not just a recycling of material that drives this aspect. Rather, it is a growing questioning of whether you should use or even create the material in the first place. On Earth right now those in industrialized areas have access to an abundance of water. What is allowed to flow down their drains in one day is often more water than those in undeveloped regions will have access to in a week. The redistribution of water is not something that can realistically occur on the physical plane. Rather, the awareness of the blessing of such abundance, followed by a deeper respect for the gifts of Gaia, will begin the growth of a Harmonic Continuum. This shift of energetic awareness creates an opportunity for a more balanced global vision of providing necessities to all beings on the planet now and in the future.

Global communication will also be brought into balance. An abundance of communication is not effective. There is much that is merely chatter and worthless words. Yet the avenue of such messaging is akin to a baby learning to use its mouth and tongue and lips. The nonsensical nature of the ideas and statements being made is like the babble of a child. As a species, the family human is in the growth mode of the fifth chakra and thus learning to communicate effectively in the new energy. Life is different now. The children born today, those we refer to as the children of the Sun, will communicate in a much faster and more effective way than you can conceive of.

Many thousands of years past, the family human was on a specific track of development. Their communication skills were of a deep, natural level. They were able to commune not just with each other but also with Gaia herself. They spoke the language of the earth, as did many other species. Theirs was a cooperative world. A strong yang occurrence — a severe solar event — shifted the humans away from such a course. Life became a struggle for survival, and the rise of yang energy was necessary for life to continue. This event brought us all into a state of imbalance. We remind you that the effect of this solar event was not only on Earth, but that is where our concern is today; therefore, we focus our words here to life on this planet. As a species, you are seeing the effects of this strong yang event on other worlds for the first time. It will be some time before the family human pieces all the information together cohesively.

Earth has been a filter for many thousands of years. We have all been volunteers in an effort to rebalance this area of the galaxy. The past 300 years have been the most difficult to endure in many ways. Now the spiral of time has reached its most tightly compressed moments. Now the spiral of time begins to release its coils. Now we all, here in the spiritual realm as well as incarnate in the physical realm, will start to feel as if there is more space to exist within. Yet there is much that must still be resolved.

How to Proceed into the Arc of the Future

To make your way into the future, you start with a deep, honest examination of your attitudes toward yin energy. How do you nurture? How do you express love to others? How far does your concern for strangers extend? How and what do you communicate to others, especially children? How and from where do you gain or access information? Remember the principle of "as you sow, so shall you reap." Apply your energy to others in the way that you would like to receive energy.

Can you stop your own voice? Can you become silent and still, deep within yourself? This lost skill is one of the primary things that keeps humanity separate from deep levels of peace and serenity.

Do you experience happiness when others feel happy? Do you love for no apparent reason, only out of principle? Are you drawn to pleasurable activities of peace and beauty?

Pressing yourself to respond in deeply honest ways will assist you to observe the spaces where yang may still be imbalanced within you. It is not a time to eliminate yang. It is a time to direct it in support of yin and thus growth for all of the family human.

This will still not be an easy path to walk. You will feel a growing sense of strength now, slight at first, but as you progress through the next decade, many tests will demonstrate your well-tempered power. You are the ones who have come through the most difficult of times. There is light now but still many stormy clouds.

Begin again if you feel you failed. You have not failed. You have held a place for growth like a dormant seed. Seek new words. Seek new ways to express yourself beyond speech. Take action. There is a time coming — and it is nearly here — when the world will talk to Gaia once more. Gaia is speaking to you now. Are you listening?

Use less. Act more. Think further ahead. Feel the earth. Be aware. Use all your senses together. Speak peaceful thoughts. Enjoy being alive.

Practice love. This will be difficult to express to everyone, but we remind you that there is no law against love. There is no cost to loving unconditionally. Love is the highest force available in the universe. It is, in a way, still undiscovered. It is not a quantifiable energy from a purely physical standpoint. We tell you now, from the realm of spirit, that the Source of all things is love. If you desire peace, practice love.

The change is in motion. Do not despair any setbacks. Love all beings. They seek to become pure energy in the same way as you. They may be imbalanced in ways. This does not make them unworthy of love. We have loved all beings through their imbalance. We send our love to the entire planet Earth at this time. Breathe love.

CHAPTER TWENTY-THREE

True Prophecy Brings Hope and Vision

As above, so below. As a spirit group, we are often looked to for guidance regarding the future. Many humans seek answers and assurances that they are on a correct path or that Earth will one day experience peace. We return the questions to you. Are you practicing true spiritual principles of love, joy, and peace? Are you actively imaging a peaceful planet and acting in accord with that concept? Since you are reading this, the answer to these questions is likely yes. We ask one more question: Are you doing enough?

Future Generations Bring Change

You might think, "Isn't this all in the hands of spirit beings?" We tell you now that you *are* spirit beings. Although you are currently incarnated in a physical form, there is much that you can and should continue to strive for in these difficult times.

The answer to the question of whether there will ever be true peace on Earth is yes. But before you get to that point, there is much that must change. This is not an easy path, and many will be tested in their spiritual resolve. Gold is purified by fire, but it is valuable only when removed from the heat. A deep purification is taking place. The cooling phase is set to begin quite soon.

In looking to the future, we see many loose threads coming together. There is no longer such a wide variety of options in what can happen on the world stage. From a purely physical perspective, this narrowing of potentials may seem restrictive. In fact, it leads to a greater liberation for the planet in the near future. For those in the spiritual realm and the spiritually minded beings incarnate on Earth, this narrowing feels like progress.

Your good spiritual work has guided and created strong channels and paths for returning energy to flow through. The world will soon feel refreshed. But first, much of the old ways of thought and belief must be brought to a conclusion. Sadly, for a short time, this means some continued violence and war. Yet even these destructive activities are being narrowed and focused. The changes being wrought are ultimately for the benefit of future generations. You could say that, in a sense, today's events are guided by those who will become future generations.

The Challenge of Prophecy and the Acceptance of Truth

Prophecy often induces fear. There is a potential for fear within these words, but we speak to you knowing you are a mature spiritual being. As such, you will remain flexible and open, using your creative abilities to continue to manifest a smooth transition through any challenges presented.

There are those who will use prophetic statements to amplify fear and gain power over others. There are those who seek to feed off of immature beings. They disguise themselves with a veneer of spirituality, but the creation of fear is the opposite of a true spiritual nature. You will know these beings by the extreme way they speak of natural changes.

For example, it is common to read about the shifting of the magnetic poles. This is a true and natural occurrence. It has happened many times in the past and will continue. It also occurs in the star called Sol. There is true science behind this relatively rare happening. It is easy to find accurate information and gain clarity. A mature spiritual person does not fear knowledge. A mature spiritual person finds little to fear at all.

There are those who attempt to profit by stirring anxiety in those who are weakened by the strong currents of change swirling around our part of the galaxy in recent decades. You do not need to hide from these changes. There is nowhere to hide from the effects of a magnetic pole shift. You not only exist on Earth, you are of Earth.

There are those who claim to live by faith but actually live by outdated dogma. In so doing, they reject much that is true and wonderful. They claim truth as their exclusive province, yet turn a blind eye toward facts. In an effort to maintain their illusions, they use fearful scenarios to control others. They often refuse to examine anything but their ancient texts, failing to recognize that those texts have been corrupted. They filter out even the basic spiritual truths of these once beautiful teachings.

Scientific explorations do not remove true spirituality. As the years progress, more accurate comprehension of the universe creates greater opportunity to consciously connect with the field of creative energy we all exist within. The great realizations of the ancient mystics are becoming science facts of the present day. This does not lessen the value of such principles; rather, it gives them strength.

You will soon see a larger understanding of the individual's role in manifesting the future. You will also see a growing global awareness of the interconnectedness of all beings. This will lead to a more balanced society in which people respect one another. Some will oppose the innate structure of such a communal approach to life, but the necessity will grow, and the most adaptable members of the family human will evolve and progress. This will not mean a loss of individuality. You will have the strength to be a being of service rather than one who seeks power.

Growing Transparency Yields a Clear Vision

The sociopolitical world will become increasingly transparent. We have long said that you can understand the changes to humanity by considering the technology of wireless communication. "Wireless communication" is a hearkening back to a time when humans were more connected with not only one another's thoughts and emotions but also the world around them. They sensed the animals, the foliage, the creatures of the sea, and even the shifting Earth. They had relationships with other nonhuman beings of intellect.

Much of this interconnection was lost through the use of indoctrination to belief systems that demanded secrecy and a hiding of truth. The family human was first taught that direct interaction with Gaia was somehow wrong and then that it was a sign of evil. Such limited thinking is opposite to the way Gaia works. It is an attempt to gain and maintain power over masses. That power is fading.

Through technology, you are witnessing more of the truth about people's struggles and desperate lives in locations around the world. People in every country now know they are not alone in their desire for stability and safety for their children. The commonality of family is becoming a global imperative. Acceptance of others is being mandated. Most greet these mandates with joy, for it is a return to the core energy of all humanity.

Much is being revealed in relation to how religions and governments manipulate data and information to control the populations. This will lead to a massive destabilization of the world society and can bring some difficulties. Understand that if there was balance present in the first place, then there could never be a toppling of such institutions.

A growing awareness of accountability will curtail the activity of those who can be considered bullies and opportunists. In fact, the age of accountability and transparency will begin to weed out many who exist in offices of public service. The exposure brought on by a growing information exchange and availability is creating a world in which there are fewer shadows. It now requires only that the population look with a keen eye to see the weakness in its society.

Remember, the majority of beings carry deep within their karmic entities a sincere desire for balance and connection. It is only those who seek power over others that cause great divisions between segments of the family human. If you are practicing awareness, you will see the chasms that have existed in the past are now mere cracks. The societies of the world are shedding their imagined differences and preparing to become a true global family once again.

Physical Earth Changes

The physical earth will continue to have major shifts. These will appear as disasters to those who are directly affected, but they are rebalancing and necessary for the future. As a species, the family human has faced climate extremes before. It is often during these times that great inner explorations are conducted and leaps of community occur. It will be the same in the near future only with this difference: The threat of mass extinction will not be present. Indeed, in the past, the majority of the population of Earth was unaware of this potential. At that time, those in the realm of spirit were most active in the realm of gravity, often taking direct action in granting succor and aid. In the coming days, those in the realm of spirit will no longer need to act in such a direct way.

There are many on the planet now and more arriving each day who possess and manifest the spiritual maturity to lead and create appropriate solutions based on the principles of love and peace. They are the messengers. It is a great achievement and represents success in the experiment of life on Earth. This opens up marvelous opportunities for the distant future. We tell you now that your view of the galaxy will be forever changed.

Peaceful Adaption to Planetary Changes

In addition to natural shifts of the physical planet, there will be a forced perspective change that will occur because of human-made challenges. Disrespect for Gaia will result in strict consequences for the family human. Ecosystems will shift away from the inclusion of humans. The earth and the biosphere will adapt to the effects of humanity's relentless actions.

The family human will struggle with this restructuring. The increased failure of the past centuries to take into account the rest of the life forms of the planet has left human life weakened and unable to rapidly shift and evolve to altered climates and food sources. Other species are adapting. Profits from creating excessive waste and squandering natural resources will weaken and fade as the generations now in the educational system gain advanced knowledge.

We tell you this not to induce fear but rather to further your personal awareness and invite you to turn your creative energies to solutions and acceptance. By denying truths or continuing to act in ways that alter the very air necessary for life, a being can slow the changes necessary for the desired future of peace on Earth.

The future requires endurance. Life on the planet always has needed patience, sometimes on a generational scale. It is time for the population to shift its vision toward the future life that will be arriving on the planet. The generations to come will marvel at the cosmos in a way that you do not yet have access to. The aspects of your spiritual nature will no longer be intellectually separated from daily life. The family human will walk the earth in awareness and wonder again.

The joy of nature will be sought as a primary element of daily living. The sense of peace among beings will be inherent in every interaction. The feeling of love will be understood at the core of all conscious beings and will be the primary drive to all actions and decisions. Can you begin today? In this way you, the spiritual being made manifest on Earth, will bring to the planet what all beings desire in their hearts.

CHAPTER TWENTY-FOUR

Chart Your Course for the Future

As above, so below. Our opening phrase indicates that there is a range of perspective available to life. From "above," the spiritual realm, we observe Earth and the planets and witness a variety of energetic activity. Our vision allows us to see the great changes and corrections occurring in this area of the galaxy. We see balance happening and welcome the process.

From the area that we indicate as "below," the physical realm, these changes and alterations to the flow of energy often look like conflict and dispute. The energy can seem erratic and discomforting. Yet there is a thread of energy that soothes those who are of a more spiritual nature. The thought that all is proceeding on a positive path of growth and harmony may not be one that is easily supported if you are looking at the events of the world, but many feel deeply that the course of life is one of hope.

From above, we now indicate that all things are in process and, despite certain events on the planet, the course of existence for the future is one of increased spirituality and balance. Yet you can see clearly that the passage to that point is not smooth or easy. Allow us to give perspective so that you can chart your personal course with confidence.

Storm-Tossed Energies

You have experienced great surges of energy. Expect more of these. To help you understand what is occurring, we will use the illustration of sailing a ship at sea. Imagine a storm at sea, and you can understand the action of the energy that is in this vicinity of the universe at the moment. You can see the storm clouds, but you are not actually within the storm. Great gusts of strong winds press against you, driving waves all about your vessel. These bursts of energy occur in varying durations and strength.

You are not headed toward a destination; you are only keeping the prow into the waves. You feel yourself rising up, and you also feel yourself sliding down. As long as you are afloat, you are fine. There is no regularity to any of this; it is just how things are going to be for a while.

To continue our seafaring illustration, imagine that you have set sail. Your maps and charts inform your decisions, but they do not tell you when the wind will blow. There may be currents and there may be flow, but the currents are not constant. A good crew on a good ship can weather storms through hard work, with focused awareness, and sometimes with luck. But you and your crew could also experience a rogue wave. A confluence of energy can create a wave that increases in an exponential way. It is higher, faster, and stronger than you would expect because of the way energy multiplies in certain situations. Minutes earlier or minutes later, you might not have that same situation; a rogue wave could not form.

In this area of the galaxy, we have much energy, and it is conflicting. It is moving in many directions, and as the energies cross, those areas that it crosses become peaks of energy. Some will feel damaged. Some will feel swept away, swept about, and pushed beyond their limits. Great energy can create, and great energy can destroy. As always, we say these things not to instill fear but to create awareness.

In this time, it is good to be still if possible. Setting a new course for your life is to set yourself inside these surges of energy. If you are in a sheltered spot, why take the risk? Yet many are already on a path of personal change and discovery. Be aware. Be mindful. If you are within the storm area, take heed and do what must be done. There is no changing the storm. There is only acceptance and inner strength. Make the best of where you are. Storms will pass. The world will attain a measure of calm. Changes are in effect now, and the peaceful future requires breaking from old karmic patterns. This, then, is the purpose of the storm.

A View of the Approaching Future

Surges of energies are going to pull and push against the fabric of society, and from above, we do not see clearly how this will finalize in this era except for this: There are new beings arriving on the planet. They have a different way of existence, and they are not subject to personal karmic echoes. They may face karmic echoes from other sources, but these new beings will face them with a different perception.

Many of you see the new ones. Understand that your generation was a bridge. Understand that you no longer are required to act in this capacity. That is the thing about being a bridge. It does not go anywhere. Once you are across, there is no reason for the bridge to continue. It only allows for safe and easier passage over rivers and ravines. The human journey is past where you began in your current incarnations. What you have accomplished is unprecedented in the recorded history of human societies. You will not be returning to the far side of the valley.

These new ones, those incarnating now, are also a bridge for their children (and their children's children) to an entirely new place for the planet. Never talk down to these new ones. They know their task from birth. Do not have any expectation for them; they are going to be human. They are going to be more human in so many ways because they have to finish processing some of the final remnants of 300 years of really, really ridiculous behavior. You have begun this process, but much of that past karmic detritus is being echoed right now. The stormy energies you are experiencing are swirling it in chaotic waves, making it difficult to navigate. The new ones arriving now are bringing a calmer way, and the settling of this karmic debris will be brought to finality within their children's lives.

These new ones can be an immediate blessing to the planet if there is openness and clean lines of thought, as well as communication around them and available to them. You see the challenge, then, that they face in current society: It is a noisy and often purposely unclear state of existence brought about by many in power. For this reason, many born today will exit soon because they cannot abide a situation in which they are not allowed to think freely. Because of their stronger energies, these ones have no choice but to think for themselves. Repression will cause an implosion. Why is there a rise in autism? Repression. Those beings are forced back into themselves. In a very real way, Earth is not ready for them. Release your expectations of them. The ones who remain on the planet are charting a new course. They inform society of a new way. They will help bridge a new path forward.

What You Can Do

What can you do now to weather this energetic shift? It is important for you to set yourself in a centered space. We ask you to use your energies of love to radiate love outward. We also ask you to radiate reason outward. Think critically. The new beings who are coming in now will respond more to reason, and the world will balance out. For now, you are in a storm.

Plans are difficult to make. In the planning phase of life, you will be blown off course. Sometimes your destination will not exist after the storm has passed. In small ways, do what is ahead of you immediately in your daily life. Look to the future, of course. You are a physical and a spiritual being, so you must look forward. But release the expectation that things will happen the way you choose. Pool your resources with others. Getting back to the illustration of the ship at sea, we recommend that you batten down the hatches to prevent yourself from being flooded. Take care of those around you, those closest to you. We are not saying, "Do not hope. Do not plan. Do not purpose. Do not move in certain ways." Understand that you will be blown off course. It is not to be taken personally. It is a large thing, globally speaking, and it is a small thing for you as an individual.

Take heed and be careful in what you dwell on. Small things can become manifest in moments of swift peak energies. As we discussed, those peak energies can come on very suddenly. Converging energies flow together very fast, and all of a sudden there is a spike of energy. If you are worried about something at the moment of that spike, you could manifest that exact thing. So it is important to make sure that your energies, your thoughts, are shifted toward positive outcomes at all times.

Life Above, Life Below

Do not be attached to life on the planet because you will be disappointed. All physical things have the same eventuality. Do not fear exiting the planet, as fear makes it harder for you to return to the realm of spirituality. What will you miss? The sooner you get through the transformation, the sooner you can witness future events. Only after you are transformed will you see things from the perspective of above.

Spiritual existence is different. There are some in the spirit realm who miss certain experiences that only occur in the realm of gravity. So we say that when you drink water, invite your spirit companions to be with you. When you hold a child, invite your companions to be with you. When you are in joy, invite your companions to be with you.

There are some in spirit who are more closely tied to the planet, and there are others who are at a greater distance. The farther you get from gravity, the greater your connection to original Source materials. The further into the gravity well, the more division, the more separation, experienced, yet we are all Source material. So the more heightened your awareness that you are

Source material, that the core energies of Source are you and everyone else, the easier it is to find balance and to deal with all the changes. The deeper the gravity well, the more ego-based personalities form. It is then that conflicts occur. We do not face challenges like that in this realm of spirit, yet we are connected to the planet, so we still deal with the repercussions of those energies and echoes.

Seek your joys. We have a different vision of this stormy energy. We see the purpose of it. We have been expecting it. Losses that you may witness on the planet are not losses from our point of view. So we do not exist in fear or in disappointment; we simply face the next surge of energy, the wave of energy, the flow of energy.

As we conclude, we always use the following words: "joy, love, peace." Those are the balancing energies. Pull those energies in. Find your peace. Find your joy. When it is necessary, let those energies back out. Let them flow through you. If you want more of them, be a conduit for them, and the universe will send those energies through you. In times of chaotic energy, it is sometimes difficult. Remember, you are dealing with a three-dimensional and a four-dimensional world, and we are speaking of things that are four and five times different dimensionally. Those energies of love, joy, and peace do not always flow freely, but they are always present. The more familiar you are with the vibrations of joy and love and peace, the more you are going to be able to access them when they are rare. Allow yourself to have joy doing what you choose to do, whatever is joyful to you, as that increases your familiarity with joy.

You seek love and joy, and in doing that, you find peace. It is that simple. And one day, all will release their hold on gravity, the things that create gravity will begin to dissipate, and things will all be the same once again. That time is far forward, and Source has much else to discover, to learn, and to create. It is a fantastic thing. Yet it all comes down to this: love, joy, and peace.

CHAPTER TWENTY-FIVE

Prophecy and a Balanced Path to the Future

As above, so below. In the realm of spiritual communication, there are several types of messages. As spiritual beings, we often seek to instruct. Within the instruction, we always attempt to include encouragement, which is the second form of the message. There is a third form of the message that we do not often engage in, and that is the work of prophesying, or the act of looking into the future.

The primary reason we do not use this form of messaging is that the energy of the times is very changeable now, and there is no clear future in sight. We do see certain markers, things that are very likely to occur, at specific moments. The details, however, do not come easily, for every choice made by humanity today is altering the patterns that in the past allowed for a clear vision of the future.

A second reason we do not use this method of communication is that it is easily misunderstood, and it tends to set people off balance in their lives. Many react with fear and seek some governmental structure, philosophical method, or organized religion to regain a sense of safety or security. By following this pattern, they are usually placing themselves outside the opportunity for true spiritual growth.

Raise Awareness of Your Time in History

We, as spiritual messengers, will often speak of awareness and the powerful energy that you individually can gain by increasing your ability to sense the complete world around you. Awareness is a key ingredient to true spirituality.

It allows you to attend to your own journey and be free of the limiting perceptions of others.

This journey through the physical realm of gravity is an important one. It is what many humans understand as life, and there is a strong belief that it is all there is to existence. The idea that death is an ending is common. Even among those who profess to believe in an afterlife, little thought is put into or few attempts are made to understand their philosophy regarding that state of being.

We speak of the conclusion of life on the planet, the end of physical existence, as a transformation, a part of a much longer journey. That journey begins before and continues past physical life. This is not a prophecy; it is a statement of knowing. Not all humans are in that state of knowledge. It is not necessary to be in agreement on this.

Increasing awareness can lead humans to a higher vibrational form of life while on the planet. Again, this does not indicate that all will agree on the proper ways to accomplish a spiritual life. However, there are many similarities to the messages of those who attain a higher vibrational consciousness. Most of those do not engage in the method of direct prophecy these days.

We tell you these things in order for you to understand that while the words that follow are in essence prophetic, for they are in regard to the future of life on Earth, they are broad based and given more to increase awareness than to create a vision. Through these words, we offer instruction in a manner, but mostly we seek to encourage and to create an opportunity for you to release fears and limitation, raising your own vibrational nature in the process.

What the Future Holds for All Humanity

The world is about to experience a cleansing. Now, understand that when we speak of this as something immediate, we are viewing this process from a higher perspective. What looks imminent to us in the realm of spirit is still several decades away for those of you on Earth. But it begins today. It has already begun.

For the past 300 years, the world has gone through the deepest transformation ever experienced in recorded history. More energetic changes and alterations have occurred in human society during this time than ever before. You are deeply affected by the past 100 years. This is the most recorded period in all of human existence. Images and writings exist that detail so much recent history of Earth that the sheer mass of information gives an illusion of importance beyond all other eras. The assigning of importance to such events as the great wars and the great, sweeping civil rights changes is a tangible daily thing. You are, in essence, still living the recent past on each day.

The shift that you will soon experience is one of filtering. The energy of the past 100 years will soon dissipate. How? In a natural way, primarily. The passing of the great populations that lived through these times is the imminent change of which we now speak. No longer will there be a need to carry the pain and hurt that was caused by these events. The world simply will cease to have a need for some of the great memorials to violence and fear, to lack and loss. The passing of the people who were directly involved will relieve the sense that these events, important as they are in human history, need to be dwelt on and pondered ceaselessly.

The lessons those times offer are from a previous vision of life on Earth. Much has changed because of those events, but there is still the tendency to apply old lessons to the new principles. This is now close to a conclusion. New lessons are being taught, and new humans are preparing the future of humanity.

Releasing the energy of retrospection will provide the opportunity to become a more forward-looking society. This will allow for a more unified approach to life on Earth. The concept of globalization will become a common way of thinking. This is not to say that countries and cultures will vanish. Far from it. The diversity of life will be embraced, celebrated, and accepted.

The concept of global unity can be approached in two ways. The first is voluntarily. The humans who will inhabit Earth post–twentieth century can choose to be in direct partnership with each other and to act in accord. Peace will be brought about by cooperative efforts. There will still be a need for commerce and trade and the legal agreements that follow these paths, but the worrisome nature of war and conquest will fade away.

The second is through global crisis. This is not ideal. However, we see that there will be an element of this in the near future. In the same way that you envision the great wars of the twentieth century, 100 years from now people will have a memory of the great restabilization of society after ecological patterns shift.

There is much talk of climate change these days. Much of the debate on the reality of such change is senseless and fueled by greed. Soon there will be no doubts about certain business practices and the imbalance they cause to the earth. Have no fear regarding the fate of the planet. Earth has taken very large hits and changes in the past, and Gaia continues along, constantly in a state of adaptation. Will humanity survive? This is the crux of the testing and filtering we have spoken of so often.

Survival in the physical realm depends on adaptation to conditions that cannot be altered. This will not be the first time that humanity has faced such a situation, but it will be the first time that so many humans can and do communicate seemingly effortlessly and instantly with one another. This potential for unified action on one another's behalf will be key to the coming shifts in geophysical patterns.

Observable Shifts in Global Patterns

Already you have witnessed offers and assistance to nations in distress from hurricanes, earthquakes, and tsunamis. Already you are observing the global society react nonviolently to aggression and revolts. There are still many areas of violence around the world, but these are increasingly isolated. The work of the global community is now often centered first on human rights and humanitarian aid. The deconstruction of old patterns will continue to be challenged, but there is a new energy that is sweeping the earth free from the imbalance of overactive yang and subjected yin.

Observe the new ways leaders of Earth's communities are speaking. Observe the new ways religious leaders are responding to scandals that once were denied or covered up. Observe the activity of women in the realm of political leadership, and see men of great power and knowledge accept their leadership.

This is the way of the future. It is a true path but not an easy one. Challenges remain. Balance is not a constant thing. Forward motion assists balance, and what we have begun to witness is just such motion. The world will not go backward.

The things that spiritually minded people have long imagined and envisioned are now coming to fruition. Future leaders of spiritual pathways will have different visions. Prophecies uttered in the future will come from a different base of existence. The reality of daily life will be fundamentally altered.

What you have asked is for Earth to exist in peace and love. These qualities will propel future societies in ways that you have not and, in truth, cannot imagine. Giving power to these changes is the spiritual quality of joy. Even though there will be challenges to life, those facing these times will be forward-thinking beings, unburdened by the past and firmly rooted in the pleasure of life and the beauty of the physical world.

In your days, then, look forward and create the prophecy of hope, kindness, and acceptance. Propel this prophecy through your practice of love, joy, and peace. The world is a fine and great place. You are fine and good beings.

Much of what we speak about here is based on having faith. We do not ask you to engage in blind faith. We ask you to increase your observational skills. Note what is right about people's actions. Make these things known to others. Use the words "love" and "joy" and "peace" often. Focus attention not on the aberrant, imbalanced randomness of the old systems of belief but rather on what is the new way, the new age of existence for the family human. In this, you will not only gain the ascension you seek but also create a true era of higher vibrational life for the future.

CHAPTER TWENTY-SIX

The Energies of Growth

As above, so below. Our purpose in communicating with you is to assist where needed, to allow for an easier passage to a higher vibrational existence, and to aid in spiritual growth. We are, in a very real sense, here to serve your needs. Although you must do your own work, we can offer guidance and advice on seeking a path to a cleaner karmic eventuality. Another way of saying this is that our guidance can make your physical lives easier.

The greeting we always offer at the opening of the channeling is an example of the way the energy of the universe works. In our communications, we often speak of the connection of things, the cause and effect of the flow of energy. Our opening phrase is a simple reminder that what occurs in the spiritual realm has a corresponding echo within the physical realm.

The actions we take in the spiritual realm are purposeful and are often designed to adjust or purify a flow of energy in the physical realm. We act, and the wave of that action can loosen energy that is blocked or entangled. To those on Earth, the effect of this action can be perceived for a great length of time as a continuing energy filter. The longer the time that passes, the more likely that same perception can become skewed and the truth or reason, the original intention of the primary action, can become lost.

There are many actions instigated in the spiritual realm for the benefit of the physical realm that have occurred throughout history. The ripples of these will interact with one another, and this can alter the original intention in unexpected and surprising ways. The disruption of patterns can be a fine thing, but patterns also serve us well if they are growth oriented. There are times when the spiritual realm must also act to quell abundant, chaotic energetic waves. In the past several hundred years, we have acted in just such a manner many times, though more often we have allowed disruption to continue, for it may create the potential of greater change in a swifter fashion. From the perspective of the beings incarnate upon the planet at that time, it can appear that chaos is being allowed at the expense of a life of peace.

We tell you now that those who participate in such great historical upheavals are chosen or choose to incarnate during these times. Their motive is pure; however, the reality of existence during great wars or plagues is far more difficult to accomplish than many understand at the time of choosing. We remind you now that death is a transition. A fully accomplished life, especially under such difficult situations, is a strong purification and escalation of energy. The karmic paths of all those affected are strengthened and heightened.

People Dealing with Difficult Circumstances

While on Earth, we are all subject to many forces that put limitations on our physical forms. This can be in the form of oppressive ruler-ships or religions. It can take the shape of difficult environmental disasters or harsh living conditions. Many experience specific physical limitations of their bodies. Missing limbs, failure of senses such as hearing or sight, the effects of diseases, whether temporary or long term, create a life with great challenges. All of these circumstances affect your perception of the world and each other. It is an easy thing to begin to feel the world is unfair or to carry a sense of bitterness about life under these conditions.

How can you alter your perceptions? Is it even necessary to do so? It may surprise some that in a karmic way, it is not necessary for a human to act in an evolved way or seek spiritual growth in each incarnation. In fact, many of those who do not act in a manner of growth are part of your daily experiences, and you must then process the energy in a specific way. You may be challenged by another being's behavior and then have the opportunity to raise the vibration of each situation you experience. Are you grateful for such challenges? Or are you perhaps the one who is creating growth-oriented challenges for others?

Spiritual growth is the path we recommend. To that end, we speak of the energies of love, joy, and peace. Generally these are a part of our closing statements in the channelings, but here we choose to explore the concepts in the light of a challenging world. To these qualities, we will also add gratitude.

These, then, are the basis for growth — not just spiritual, but also mental, emotional, and physical to varying degrees. In your life, whatever the situation you find yourself engaged in, these qualities can improve your vision and perception, if only by small increments. Growth is measured in many ways. Sometimes the most minute adjustment in attitude or acceptance will create a ripple effect that can result in a wave of change that will significantly alter the future.

It is important to know that there are no opposites for these energies. There is no opposite to love, joy, peace, or gratitude. There is only lack of those energies. Dualism is not how the universe works. It may at first appear that hate, depression, fear, or thanklessness are the opposites of these energies, but they are not energies at all. To foster hatred is to deprive the world of the energy of love. To be in a state of depression is to be without access to joy. To experience fear is to know lack of peace. To be thankless is to fail to see the flow of energy available at varying levels to all beings. The vacuum these words represent can be filled.

If you find that you have accepted a dualistic vision of the world, you will also find that you are, on some level, placing yourself in a position of judgment. This is a hard thing to overcome, especially if life is difficult for you as an individual. There can be a fair amount of pain in a person's life. This can and often does lead to a lack of growth-based energies. It is said that fear is pain borrowed from the future, and anger is pain carried from the past. To a great extent, this is a true statement.

Patterns of pain, especially emotional and mental, can be the most difficult to shift, purify, and alter. They can affect the physical form in crippling ways. When loved ones are taken away from you accidentally or violently, the pain can be nearly intolerable and is sometimes more than a being can bear. But if you can access the energy of love in those moments, if you can reach outside of your pain and draw the love you felt for the one now lost closer to your karmic core, swift healing of the heart can occur. This energy can and will radiate outward and affect others near you.

In moments of great loss or deep personal challenge, it is easy to cast the world in dualistic ways. If the challenge is perceived as created by another person, it can be difficult to see that that person is also an affected being who lacks the energies of love, joy, peace, and gratitude. The imbalance is the result of an inability to gain the growth energies necessary to create a spiritual existence. This does not excuse that person's actions. It does provide an opportunity for those who interact with him or her to channel growth energy toward such a state of lack.

Open Yourself to Growth

When you channel these energies of growth, when you allow them to flow through your being, they will nourish and enrich your life, both while you are on the planet and also in a karmic way. By allowing the energies of growth, you are acting as a conduit and offering to spread it for the benefit of other beings. Your physical situation may not change, but it can become easier to carry on in the face of difficult times.

Make no mistakes about our message. We seek to improve where possible, and this information is the most fundamental of principles we can offer. Those who allow this knowledge to become a part of their patterns and actions will find life is more pleasant and holds more opportunities than they may have once believed.

Allowing the sense of judgment to melt away is a key ingredient in preparing for your growth. It opens the path not for just yourself but for all beings alive now and in the future. Releasing judgment will allow a power to flow through you that filters away other imbalances.

We said earlier that it is not necessary to seek spiritual growth in every aspect of your karmic existence. We now ask, why would you choose to take such a path? Why choose lack rather than love? What is the gain in remaining caught in patterns of the past?

Strengthen yourselves today by choosing the path of growth. It is as simple as accepting the reminder that true spirituality is found in the display of the qualities of love, joy, and peace. Be grateful for the opportunity to be alive, if only for a short time, even if your life is limited compared to others. Acting with gratitude brings the potential for spiritual growth.

CHAPTER TWENTY-SEVEN

How to Keep Peace in Difficult Times

As above, so below. It is a fair question for a spiritually minded individual to ask why seemingly bad things happen when you are taking what you believe to be the best and highest path. Why do adverse events arrive in your life when you are doing your best to follow a course of spiritual work? Some may even begin to feel they are wrong in some sense.

There are reactions that can and do occur when the world seems to turn against your personal path of growth. Disease, economic difficulties, or chaotic environments can draw your once high-vibrational existence down into a first chakra style of living. You may become angry or fearful, struggling to regain the balance you once felt was secure. Let us consider a straightforward and clear vision of the current times and explore options that are available.

Being Human

Many of these challenges arise simply because you are a human being. Being such, you must deal with other human beings and the choices they make under pressures that everyone faces when incarnate.

Though all beings have access to higher vibrational existence, not all beings have the opportunity of a clear spiritual path. Many are struggling with wars, famines, droughts, and diseases brought on by poor living conditions or a lack of adequate health care. In stable countries, people have easier lives that allow for more freedom to pursue spiritual goals. But even in those conditions, situations can occur that create stress and result in lower vibrational actions.

In many cases, it is the proximity of people that causes stress and creates psychic pressure. Those of you who are of a higher vibration sense this psychic stress deeply, and it often causes you to feel violated in your physical life. Psychic stress exists for all beings. It is only those with a higher vibrational level that will be aware of it and understand that a core energy lacks balance in their physical and emotional worlds. Gaining and maintaining balance are difficult in challenging times. Yet only by remaining centered within your own personal peace will you find the strength to continue your growth.

It is said that time heals all wounds, but that is not often a comfort when you are facing severe stress. We often say that the future will be better. This is true. Getting past psychic stress requires endurance on the part of the individual being. It also requires commitment to a higher path, one of spiritually based activity. That higher path can offer a perspective that many on the planet do not currently share or are even aware of in a conscious way. That higher perspective of spirituality allows us to see past lives and into the future. We are able to see the progress of human societies with greater clarity.

Karma

When it comes to karma, understand that not many of those alive today are coming from a peaceful series of past lives. More often than not, especially for those born in the last fifty or sixty years, the karmic lineage is one of battles and violence. The great wars fought just prior to the 1600s and on through the twentieth century left a swath of imbalanced energy that manifests today as anger and fear even when the stream of time indicates abundance and freedom. It is precisely this imbalance that the more spiritually minded beings, those aware of their higher selves and seeking a purer vibration, are here to balance out.

That balance is not achieved by returning to the energy of battle. Many of you may, in your deep core selves, feel that you want to fight an injustice or right a wrong or simply defend yourself, your family, or your possessions when someone with a lack of balance appears to confront you. These are testing times, and you must not feel that you have failed if your desire for battle rises. You all were once warriors. In the same manner, you all were once victims of war.

The people of Earth see clearly that battle and destruction are not valid paths for any society, yet they continue to engage in such action. Why? The old patterns are shifting and changing, but it is a time-based change. There is much to rebalance, and it is difficult to not react to perceived attacks in an equal fashion. "Seek peace in all things" is our advice, but it is not always possible. Do you then take up arms? Join a militia? That is a choice, and in some cases, taking the warrior's path is a true and strong expression of a rebalancing of energy. There are other ways.

Seeking peace is often about creating community. When you see the word "community," do you also see the word "commune" or "communication"? Yet some refuse to listen or reason. In the cases you are able to, walk away. Do not engage. If you press against them, you are also propping them up. If you allow no support and give no purchase, sooner or later the energy and momentum will come to an end.

In the case of an inexorable advance of military might, you must understand that your time on the planet is limited no matter what. Clinging to life is a deep-seated drive. A person with a higher vibrational vision will see further than this incarnation. Maintaining your peace internally may be tested in such extreme cases. Seek the most peaceful path available. If it means closing down to outside influences, then reach deep and access the core energy of your higher self. From certain points of view, this is not optimal, and we agree. Yet it is the cost of being a human on Earth.

It is getting better. Societies are shifting to more communication between people rather than among governments. It is here that neighborhoods become something beyond simple geographic location. They become communities. It is here that the youth and their children are changing the world to a more peaceful place.

Health and Vitality

We can again see that "being human" is also the simplest answer to the question of why a person contracts a disease or has a disability. Humanity has made many advances regarding health and care. They have also created a food supply unequaled at any other time in history. That it is not distributed equally is a course that can and will be corrected in the near future.

The unfortunate byproduct of this increased supply of goods is that there are now health risks endemic in the food industry. This has been an ongoing shift for over one hundred years. Now new knowledge is being gained, and a clear sight of how the human body is unable to adapt to many of these changes is strengthening a growing movement toward greater health. What you deal with in the present day, however, is the culmination of many years of your, your parents', or your grandparents' eating, drinking, or smoking artificial things that once were deemed safe and even touted as healthier than the natural foods that humanity thrived on for tens of thousands of years. You can return to more natural ways, but in many cases, the damage is already accomplished. Genetically, the succeeding generations can and will alter the highly resilient human body to a stronger course.

In the meantime, when you are afflicted with a physically challenging existence, remember that time on Earth is finite. It is better to enjoy quality of life than to worry about its length. Seek a life without pain and suffering. Do not remain attached to a course that drains your energy and that of your loved ones. The spiritually minded person will know intuitively that the tribes of old understood the cycle of life and death and cooperated with it rather than seeking to subvert nature.

We are not saying that it is appropriate to end your life at the first sign of struggles. These struggles are a part of the filter of life on the planet. You are being asked to find balance in the situation.

The Balance of Peace

Seeking peace in a confrontation may not always be successful, but at least you did not prolong the confrontation. By seeking joy under physically trying times, you shift away from the pain that life can bring and act to regain the focus of spirituality in it. Understand that once you pass from the planet, you may soon return again and face new pressures and challenges. This, then, is the work of a spiritually minded being.

Why do we all do this? This is a deeper question that we may ponder in solitary silences and darkened spaces. The answer that we can give is: We do this for love. The energy of the universe, the source of all existence, is seeking new ways and paths to express itself. In so doing, Source faces moments when the paths are difficult and imbalances occur. It is not that Source has made a mistake; it is that Source energy is trying to spread the flow of creativity and growth in new and unique ways. Some experiments do not flow freely at the beginning. Most require adjustments in the process.

This locality of the universe is undergoing a very strong adjustment period. The end result is in sight. The world is gaining an altered future. In the recent past, all prophecy pointed to a perilous and disastrous course for the human race. Together, we have shifted that energy to one of growth, but the changes that would have occurred through violence must still occur in some form. The difference is you are now moving toward the future in the shadow of loving energy. Stressful times are upon you all. It is your choice to respond differently and to set a new course for humanity.

In all things, then, first and foremost seek love. It is the core energy of Source, and it will not fail.

CHAPTER TWENTY-EIGHT

A Generation of Balance and Growth Approaches

As above, so below. It is a time of testing. It is a time of purification. It is a time unlike any other in recorded history. A generation that was born into a world of vast information gathering and dissemination is coming to maturity. The children nearing adulthood now have at their fingertips more knowledge than existed in previous centuries. They also are tracked and observed more closely than any previous generation could imagine. What is the result of such intense scrutiny? What is the potential with the availability of such abundant information? Let us look forward to see the ramifications of the energy of the present.

Everything Is Energy

The universe is made up of energetic aspects with the ability to combine into an infinite diversity of existence. From the subatomic charges to the galactic clusters, everything moves in spirals and cycles of waves. Each aspect of energy acts in some way on all other aspects. In many cases, the action is subtle, but as objects become proximate, the increasing energetic ties gain complexity.

Here on planet Earth, the growing population, combined with increasing technologies, has brought all beings into a tight and sometimes cramped state of existence. The result is confusing for many who were born and raised in the twentieth century. It can be chaotic to those who were not born into this fast-moving weave of communication and potential expansion. Why do we say "potential"? Is the world not shifting and altering in the present day? Yes, it is, but this is all in preparation for something truly phenomenal.

In the latter part of the twentieth century, several harmonizing events occurred. They are loosely known as the Convergence, the Concordance, and the Coalescence. We might also say that they represent a greater awakening to humanity's spiritual connection. For many people, these events created an expectation to achieve a higher state of evolution or consciousness. Those beings are now reaching the end of their physical course.

The expectation of greater spiritual focus may seem to be delayed. At this time, we see many wondering what it was all about, what the purpose of life is, and whether or not they succeeded in raising the vibration of the planet.

It is possible to look at the conflicts that are taking place and believe that humankind may never rise above primitive warlike action and that nothing has improved. We tell you now that the reaction you are a witness to these days is an ending of old structures. The old energy is roiling and seeking old pathways. Those pathways no longer exist, and thus that old energy is flowing into newer, narrower channels, giving the appearance that this old energy has great strength and speed. It also seems as if there is so much of it that it occasionally overflows its banks. Soon, however, the flow will grow steadier, then weaker, and shortly after that, the energy will be purified and channeled to a greater purpose, one of harmony and true expansion of humanity's potential.

Our Children's Children

The last generations coming of age in the twentieth century created an environment where everything could be questioned, from great political and religious structures to the way an individual human thought or felt about life. Those questions had answers, and by gaining the answers, humanity did what it always does: It found a more efficient path. The open arena of questioning cannot be closed now. There is too much freedom inherent in the mass communication of life today. This is a strength for the future generations.

Those coming to maturity within the next decade know no other way. It is their personal reality; thus, it will grow and continue, for the majority of the world's youth believe in this openness and freedom of choice.

They also face an internal challenge. They were born into a world of violent sneak attacks resulting in an environment where everyone falls under suspicion. They are offered the great gift of speedy and efficient travel and then are placed under harsh restriction. The vast array of communication possibilities is also an untrustworthy field of rumor and falsehood. And they are weary of living beneath such stress.

Each generation seems to feel in opposition to the one prior. One generation may eschew material goods and wealth, and the next gathers possessions hungrily, seeking to obtain and control much by way of physical goods. Just as the previous generations sought freedoms and rights for all beings, succeeding generations will bring a tighter control to the world. Ultimately, this does not mean a loss of freedoms; rather, it puts focus on the rights of all humans and coordinates the flow of energy to equality.

In the very near future, the question of race or gender simply will never again be an issue. Indeed, the generation that follows those reaching maturity today will be hard-pressed to understand why there was any discrimination at all. This is an aspect of the retention of freedoms gained.

They will also require greater control over borders and intention of travel. This is the world that is being created today. It will not be about restriction. It will be about appropriate behavior and the ability for all beings on Earth to have what they need in their places of birth or national origin. It is born of mistrust, but it will blossom as the quality of self-discipline.

There will be a greater opening of information to all the world society. Concepts of health and disease prevention will be freely available and not soaked in old superstition or dogma. The ability to create an economic base that does not require a commitment to a large corporation will become a standard way of development for many of the peoples in underdeveloped regions. Distribution of goods and services will attain new levels of balance and fairness, granting a growing freedom from a ruling class.

This future will be what many have desired for decades and envisioned as a potential for the world. It will not be exactly what they have wished for or understood as an appropriate reality. From the standpoint of the past few generations, there may seem to be more restrictions than necessary. From the perspective of those who will develop this society, all the things that appear to be restrictions will actually form the guidelines and networks that allow peace and prosperity to flow evenly throughout the planet.

Those of the last generations of the twentieth century can feel confident that all their efforts in seeking a peaceful planet are yielding results. There is no delay. Despite the events taking place in the current age, the lessons being internalized by the upcoming generations are deep and positive and will motivate an equality that will benefit humanity in a way currently unimaginable to those in a passing reality.

The conclusion of that generation — the one alive today, those remnants of the past century — will be a signal. The great reduction of the world population will free up resources of energy that will fuel the great imminent changes to future human society. With that release, the setting for the twenty-second century can begin. It will be vastly different from what you may expect. It is this new world to which you will return to resume your karmic growth.

The Reality of the Future

This next generation is less concerned with spiritual matters and exploration than previous ones. This is because they are already in a strong state of acceptance and intuitive action. They were born into a world in which what was once thought of as mystical is increasingly considered common knowledge. Their concerns are more physical: clarifying the lines of communication, establishing cooperative and respectful borders, and living in full balance with Gaia's natural ways. Once these matters are fully healed and revitalized, the following generations can begin the spiritual exploration that will flood the earth with a knowledge of creation and life that will surpass all the information at hand today.

The weight of such data and the intensity of the scrutiny on the youth currently alive are of little matter to them in the broader scope of their lives. Despite being more physically directed, they take great joy in the new paths of communication available and the constant conversations they engage in. A balance is coming in this regard, but for the time being, it is new and they are excited about what they can do.

Far from being disturbed by the prospect of surveillance, they sense the potential for greater peace in a troubled world. They learn their boundaries within this reality, but they also learn what is necessary and what is not. Already they seek to adjust the new patterns of peacekeeping to be more in line with what they envision to be the necessary future of Earth's societies.

These ones will love the world differently. They are passionate in many ways, but it is not always demonstrated in the same manner as humans did in the recent past. It is not their way. Theirs is not the way of the generation that prepared this world for them. It is a new way. It is the future.

CHAPTER TWENTY-NINE

A True Path of Spiritual Ascension

As above, so below. For the spiritually aware being, these are interesting days. There is much that has shifted and continues to adjust. You are seeing random actions that force you to stop and consider what path humanity is actually on. There are times when spiritually aware beings wonder whether there truly is a rising vibration or an increase of spiritual energy on the planet. There are days when the evidence supporting this is sparse.

We offer you an assurance that, in many ways, you must either take on faith or reject wholly: The nature of the planet and all the beings upon it is moving toward increased peace and balance. You can conceive of this vision, so you know that it is possible. But when will Earth get there?

Two Traditional Spiritual Paths

There are two traditional spiritual paths on Earth. In recorded history, the one that is most often associated with spirituality is the path of ascension, which is looking beyond a mere physical life to a time when a person is in a heavenly realm and close to God in whatever way that society envisions a deity and afterlife. There is much that is right about this path. However, in the present day, there is a great imbalance in the practicality of looking only to heaven.

The second path is one that is more natural for the family human to follow. It is the path that has a longer history than can be proven through written or recorded history. Many follow it closely today, but they remain quiet in their practices. This is the path of descension, that is, the way of walking the earth in great harmony and close partnership. It is a powerful physical path that connects to the realm of gravity in a primal way. Both paths are valuable. We will discuss them separately and allow you to find your own way.

There is extreme imbalance in the path of ascension today that is causing much of the random violence and havoc on Earth. This is not an energy that can be easily corrected. Many believers take this path. To some, it may seem a good thing. The reality is that many do not truly believe what they have been taught or profess to believe. They are simply accepting ancient mythologies. They do not question the course.

However, those who follow others without critically assessing their message abdicate personal responsibility in an attempt to attain a higher vibration. By following others, they fail to have a true spiritual experience. Such beings act thoughtlessly, saying and doing only what they have been told is acceptable. They remain spiritually immature, allowing others to "feed" and "carry" them through life. They place faith in a future of ascension but have no true personal vision. When the end of life nears, such believers may begin a quest for answers. This is often done out of fear, for they have not developed abilities that allow them to attain a truly ascendant course and pass from the planet in a high level of spiritual peace.

Correct Imbalance on Your Path

True ascendency is not a group path; it is an individual path. You cannot follow anyone else's path and succeed on your own. Religions may appear to be ascendant in their approach and often speak of higher spiritual realms. However, the reality is that they lower your spiritual nature to cast the illusion of ascension. If you are seeking to raise your vibration — that is, to attain a higher spiritual nature while in the realm of gravity — you cannot be attached to another physical being's personal vision. Even if the vision is good and true, it is not completely valid for another person. Spirituality is not a one-size-fits-all course. There are things in the universe that remain essentially true, but in many ways, there is no absolute truth that must be followed, at least not one that can be fully grasped by those in the physical realm at this time.

Correcting imbalance is difficult on a global scale. Changing the minds of millions of blind followers is like changing the course of a river. It is easier to correct imbalance on an individual level.

To begin is simple. First ask, "Why do I believe what I believe?" At this point, the task becomes more difficult for two reasons: First, you must know what you believe. Many have been following a religion for much of their lives and may have even taken some instruction in their youth, but they likely have forgotten much of that instruction or have heard certain words and concepts repeated so often that they believe these ideas come from within themselves. Taking an inventory of one's beliefs is a good spiritual exercise. It requires the beliefs to stand up to scrutiny. If they fail to do so, ask yourself, "If not these concepts, then what?" Once you have an account of your belief system, you then face a second difficulty: acknowledging that your actions and current path may not be leading you to a higher vibrational existence. Within this second difficulty, there are two blocks: the ego, which cannot admit to an imbalanced course, and tribal pressure, which hinders you from going against what is accepted by everyone around you. Family and friends may be well meaning in trying to hold you to an ancient course of belief. It may be their path, but it is not necessarily yours.

There is only a personal path to higher vibrational existence. No one comes into or passes from the planet in the same way. No two people, not even twins (no matter how similar), can follow the exact same path through life. No one, not even those who perish together in a tragic event, passes into the realm of spirit with anyone else. Your spiritual growth can be shared on some levels. Stories and experiences can be exchanged in a communal setting. Yet these are not things that can be duplicated. Each spiritual experience is unique. Each human life is unique. This is a fundamental reason for life on the planet.

The path to ascend, to raise your vibration to attain a spiritual existence, is valid and one that carries great rewards. The truth is it is much easier to do this than all the teachings of all the religions of history make it seem.

Many have subverted the process of ascension in an effort to create empires and kingdoms for themselves. The accumulation of wealth often becomes more valued than the spiritual growth of the followers. People set themselves up as leaders and authorities and then indoctrinate followers, often through various forms of coercion, to structured teachings. These teachings are designed to keep people under control by eliminating freethinking and thus from seeking personal spiritual experiences. A person's livelihood might depend on professing loyalty to a belief system, and sometimes people risk their lives when they fail to submit to religion.

Although much of this energy remains, a great awakening is underway. This is made possible by the vast amount of information available to nearly all of the family human. Now more than ever, people are free to ask questions and share concerns about old mythologies. This is the beginning of the path to ascension. If you are reading these words, you are likely following the path of true spirituality.

Two Paths Become One

Becoming aware of your world, taking full opportunity to experience the physical realm in all its beauty and diversity, and learning the ways and principles of life on the planet are the very first steps to gaining a higher spiritual vibration.

Here we see how the secondary path of descension is not at all separate from a true spiritual experience. This path of deepening a person's relationship with Earth can be limiting when one does not acknowledge the principle "as above, so below." If a person believes that everything that happens in a human lifetime is the limit for that entity, a great opportunity is missed.

Walking a natural earthbound path becomes more expansive when you acknowledge the principle "as above, so below." A greater experience is available as a person witnesses the interconnectedness of life. When you comprehend the inherent energy that passes through all life, when you begin to observe the effect you can have on society by raising your level of awareness and expressing your love outward, you align yourself with larger forces. Although a true spiritual path is a personal one, it is important to understand the balance that human beings can achieve together.

Action in this way will bring you a greater sense of wholeness that is a marker of true spirituality. Here is where you begin to fully sense the connection to the Source of all energy of the universe. Here is where you begin to understand the true nature of the concept of a deity. It is here that you realize there is no need for a mediator, a priest, or a priestess to intercede on your behalf.

This is where the true spiritual seeker feels the natural rise in vibration and embraces the lofty concept that he or she is an aspect of what others refer to as God. As a spiritual seeker, you learn that your personal responsibilities include all those attributes that are called "godly" by others. The reality is that these are inherent in each member of the family human. Any aberration from true spiritual concepts can be attributed to the imbalanced vision of separate heavens and gods that dominate societies to this day. Any action taken by a religion that is not motivated by love, joy, and peace is a clear indication that such a belief system is no longer relevant to the increasing global awareness of true spirituality.

Using the principles of love, joy, and peace in all aspects of life is the way of future societies. You are beginning to see this more and more in individuals all across the globe. This will soon increase in a dramatic way.

We said earlier that much of what we speak about here requires faith. We do not ask you to engage in blind faith. We ask you to increase your observational skills. Note what is right about people's actions. Make these things known to others. Use the words "love" and "joy" and "peace" often. Focus attention not on the aberrant, imbalanced randomness of the old systems of belief but rather on what is the new way, the new age of existence for the family human. In this, you will not only gain the ascension you seek but also create a true era of higher vibrational life for the future.

About the Author

Author and channel Jeff Michaels has agreed to be the voice for Onereon: a warm, insightful, and compassionate "human resource" group here to assist us as we navigate the current waves of energy. Above all else, the Onereon group believes in us and our ability to grow and evolve. Much of what they say is indicative of the future of humanity and the vitality of the planetary system that we are a part of. *How to Become the True You* is Jeff's fifth collection of channeled articles. Other titles include *Harmonic Coalescence: The Future of Humanity*, *Touch the Earth: A Path to Ascension*, *Beings: A Journey to Joy*, and *Light: The Reason for Existence.*

Jeff Michaels is on a lifelong path of service with more than thirty years of experience in ministry, energy work, writing, teaching, and personal intuitive consulting. He is committed to guiding others to follow their personal paths to their highest potentials. To learn more, please visit www.Quintessence1.com.

Light Technology PUBLISHING **Presents**

Tina Louise Spalding

Great Minds Speak to You

"Many in spirit look on these times of difficulty, abundance, trouble, and innovation and wish to share with you their experiences and ideas. Some famous names and faces will come to mind as you read this book, and you will glean some fine information about their own learning, their own suffering, and indeed their own experience in the life after this life, for they all wish to tell you that there is no death as you perceive it to be. They are all there in their astral forms, enjoying their continued growth, their continued expansion, and their continued joy in living."

— Ananda

Chapters Include:

- Albert Einstein
- Jerry Garcia
- Marilyn Monroe
- John Huston
- Amy Winehouse
- Princess Diana
- Elizabeth Taylor
- John and Robert Kennedy
- Michael Jackson
- Cecil B. DeMille
- Pablo Picasso
- Queen Mother Elizabeth
- George Bernard Shaw
- John Lennon
- Jesus Christ

$19.95 Softcover, 192 pp.
ISBN 978-1-62233-010-2

CD of Live Channelings Included!

Making Love to GOD
The Path to Divine Sex

"We are here to teach the way to divine bliss, and we know you are scared — scared to lie naked caressing your lover with rapt attention and honor. Give love all day, and you will be guaranteed to receive love all night. The divine sexual experience connects you, God, and your lover — if you have one — together in a dance of divine bliss."

— Ananda

Topics Include:

- How We Came to Misunderstand Sexual Energy
- Using Divine Sex Energy
- Specific Steps and Sensations
- Blocks to Transformation
- A Transformed View of Sex and Sexual Energy
- Following the Path to Transformation
- Reaping the Harvest

$19.95 Softcover, 416 pp.
ISBN 978-1-62233-009-6

Print Books: Visit Our Online Bookstore www.LightTechnology.com
eBooks Available on Amazon, Apple iTunes, Google Play, and Barnes & Noble

Light Technology PUBLISHING Presents

THE ANCIENT SECRET OF THE FLOWER OF LIFE, VOLUME 1

Once, all life in the universe knew the Flower of Life as the creation pattern, the geometrical design leading us into and out of physical existence. Then from a very high state of consciousness, we fell into darkness, the secret hidden for thousands of years, encoded in the cells of all life.

Now, we are rising from the darkness, and a new dawn is streaming through the windows of perception. This book is one of those windows. Drunvalo Melchizedek presents in text and graphics the Flower of Life workshop, illuminating the mysteries of how we came to be.

Sacred geometry is the form beneath our being and points to a divine order in our reality. We can follow that order from the invisible atom to the infinite stars, finding ourselves at each step. The information here is one path, but between the lines and drawings lie the feminine gems of intuitive understanding.

You may see them sparkle around some of these provocative ideas:

- Remembering our ancient past
- The secret of the Flower unfolds
- The darker side of our present/past
- The geometries of the human body
- The significance of shape and structure

$25.00 Softcover, 240 PP.
ISBN 978-1-891824-17-3

Drunvalo Melchizedek's life experience reads like an encyclopedia of breakthroughs in human endeavor. He studied physics and art at the University of California at Berkeley, but he feels that his most important education came after college. In the past twenty-five years, he has studied with over seventy teachers from all belief systems and religious understandings. For some time now, he has been bringing his vision to the world through the Flower of Life program and the Mer-Ka-Ba meditation. This teaching encompasses every area of human understanding, explores the development of humankind from ancient civilizations to the present time, and offers clarity regarding the world's state of consciousness and what is needed for a smooth and easy transition into the twenty-first century.

Print Books: Visit Our Online Bookstore www.LightTechnology.com
eBooks Available on Amazon, Apple iTunes, Google Play, and Barnes & Noble

Light Technology PUBLISHING Presents

THE ANCIENT SECRET OF THE FLOWER OF LIFE, VOLUME 2

The sacred Flower of Life pattern, the primary geometric generator of all physical form, is explored in even more depth in this volume, the second half of the famed Flower of Life workshop. The proportions of the human body; the nuances of human consciousness; the sizes and distances of the stars, planets, and moons; and even the creations of humankind are all shown to reflect their origins in this beautiful and divine image. Through an intricate and detailed geometrical mapping, Drunvalo Melchizedek shows how the seemingly simple design of the Flower of Life contains the genesis of our entire third-dimensional existence.

From the pyramids and mysteries of Egypt to the new race of Indigo children, Drunvalo presents the sacred geometries of the reality and the subtle energies that shape our world. We are led through a divinely inspired labyrinth of science and stories, logic and coincidence, on a path of remembering where we come from and the wonder and magic of who we are.

Finally, for the first time in print, Drunvalo shares the instructions for the Mer-Ka-Ba meditation, step-by-step techniques for the re-creation of the energy field of the evolved human, which is the key to ascension and the next dimensional world. If done from love, this ancient process of breathing prana opens up for us a world of tantalizing possibility in this dimension, from protective powers to the healing of oneself, of others, and even of the planet.

Topics Include:

- The Unfolding of the Third Informational System
- Whispers from Our Ancient Heritage
- Unveiling the Mer-Ka-Ba Meditation
- Using Your Mer-Ka-Ba
- Connecting to the Levels of Self
- Two Cosmic Experiments
- What We May Expect in the Forthcoming Dimensional Shift

$25[00] Softcover, 272 PP.
ISBN 978-1-891824-21-0

Light Technology PUBLISHING Presents

THE BOOK OF transformation

THROUGH ROBERT SHAPIRO

Topics Include:

Heart Love/Heart Heat • Benevolent Magic • Living Prayer
Disentanglement • Deep Disentanglement
Disentanglement Clearings • and much more!

— Learn how to ask for clearing of old traumas and discomforts.

— Learn how to create a nourishing, benevolent life for yourself and others.

eBook ONLY $2.99

with CD

$17.95 Plus Shipping

ISBN 13: 978-1-891824-70-8
Softcover 224 PP.
6 X 9 Perfect Bound

Shifting Frequencies

Sounds for Vibratory Activation

by Jonathan Goldman

For the first time, Healing Sounds pioneer Jonathan Goldman tells us about shifting frequencies — how to use sound and other modalities to change vibrational patterns for both personal and planetary healing and transformation. Through his consciousness connection to Shamael, angel of sound, Jonathan shares his extraordinary scientific and spiritual knowledge and insights, providing information, instructions, and techniques on using sound, light, color, visualization, and sacred geometry to experience shifting frequencies. The material in this book is both timely and vital for health and spiritual evolution.

Chapters Include:

- Sound Currents: Frequency and Intent
- Vibratory Resonance
- Vocalization, Visualization, and a Tonal Language
- The Harmonics of Sound
- Vocal Harmonics and Listening
- Energy Fields

In this book, you will:

- explore the use of sound in ways you never imagined for healing and transformation
- discover harmonics as a key to opening to higher levels of consciousness
- learn about the angel chakra and what sounds may be used to activate this new energy center
- find out how to transmute imbalanced vibrations using your own sounds
- experience the secrets of crystal singing

Print Books: Visit Our Online Bookstore www.LightTechnology.com
eBooks Available on Amazon, Apple iTunes, Google Play, and Barnes & Noble

Light Technology PUBLISHING Presents

Shamanic Secrets Mastery Series

Speaks of Many Truths, Zoosh, and Reveals the Mysteries through Robert Shapiro

This book explores the heart and soul connection between humans and Earth. Through that intimacy, miracles of healing and expanded awareness can flourish. To heal the planet and be healed as well, you can lovingly extend your energy self out to the mountains and rivers and intimately bond with Earth. Gestures and vision can activate your heart to return you to a healthy, caring relationship with the land you live on. The character of some of Earth's most powerful features is explored and understood with exercises given to connect you with those places. As you project your love and healing energy there, you help Earth to heal from human destruction of the planet and its atmosphere. Dozens of photographs, maps, and drawings assist the process in twenty-five chapters, which cover Earth's more critical locations.

ISBN 978-1-891824-12-8 • Softcover, 528 pp. • $19.95

Learn to understand the sacred nature of your physical body and some of the magnificent gifts it offers you. When you work with your physical body in these new ways, you will discover not only its sacredness but its compatibility with Mother Earth, the animals, the plants, and even the nearby planets, all of which you now recognize as being sacred in nature. It is important to feel the value of oneself physically before you can have any lasting physical impact on the world. If a physical energy does not feel good about itself, it will usually be resolved; other physical or spiritual energies will dissolve it because they are unnatural. The better you feel about your physical self when you do the work in the first book, as well as this one and the one to follow, the greater and more lasting the benevolent effect will be on your life, on the lives of those around you, and ultimately on your planet and universe.

ISBN 978-1-891824-29-6 • Softcover, 576 pp. • $25.00

Spiritual mastery encompasses many different means to assimilate and be assimilated by the wisdom, feelings, flow, warmth, function, and application of all beings in your world who you will actually contact in some way. A lot of spiritual mastery has been covered in different bits and pieces throughout all the books we've done. My approach to spiritual mastery, though, will be as grounded as possible in things that people on Earth can use — but it won't include the broad spectrum of spiritual mastery, like levitation and invisibility. My life is basically going to represent your needs, and in a story-like fashion it gets out the secrets that have been held back."

— Speaks of Many Truths

ISBN 978-1-891824-58-6 • Softcover, 720 pp. • $29.95

Light Technology PUBLISHING Presents

David K. Miller

FIFTH-DIMENSIONAL SOUL PSYCHOLOGY

The basic essence of soul psychology rests with the idea that the soul is evolving and that part of this evolution is occurring through incarnations in the third dimension. Now, to even speak about the soul evolving is perhaps a controversial subject because we know that the soul is eternal. We know that the soul has been in existence for infinity, and we know that the soul is perfect. So why would the soul have to evolve?

The answer to this question is complex, and we may not be able to totally answer it using third-dimensional terminology. But it is an important question to answer, because the nature of soul evolution is inherently connected to your experiences in the third dimension. The soul, in completing its evolutionary journey, needs these experiences in the third dimension, and it needs to complete the lessons here.

—Vywamus

$16.95 • Softcover • 288 PP. • 6 X 9 Perfect Bound • ISBN 978-1-62233-016-4

OTHER BOOKS BY DAVID K. MILLER

1 

2 

3 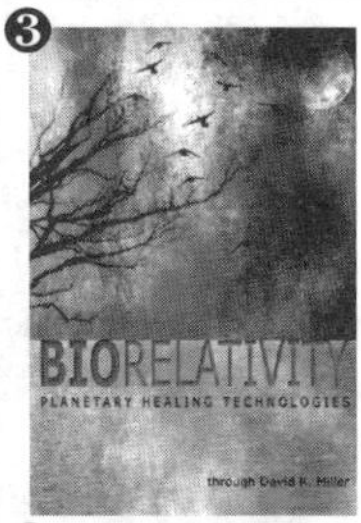

4 

5 

6 

7 

8 

9 

1. **Arcturians: How to Heal, Ascend, and Help Planet Earth**
   $16.95 • 352 PP. • SOFTCOVER • 978-1-62233-002-7
2. **Kaballah and the Ascension**
   $16.95 • 176 PP. • SOFTCOVER • 978-1-891824-82-1
3. **Biorelativity: Planetary Healing Technologies**
   $16.95 • 352 PP. • SOFTCOVER • 978-1-891824-98-2
4. **Raising the Spiritual Light Quotient**
   $16.95 • 384 PP. • SOFTCOVER • 978-1-891824-89-0
5. **Connecting with the Arcturians**
   $17.00 • 256 PP. • SOFTCOVER • 978-1-891824-94-4
6. **New Spiritual Technology for the Fifth-Dimensional Earth**
   $19.95 • 240 PP. • SOFTCOVER • 978-1-891824-79-1
7. **Teachings from the Sacred Triangle, Vol. 1**
   $16.95 • 292 PP. • SOFTCOVER • 978-0-971589-43-8
8. **Teachings from the Sacred Triangle, Vol. 2**
   $16.95 • 254 PP. • SOFTCOVER • 978-1-891824-19-7
9. **Teachings from the Sacred Triangle, Vol. 3**
   $16.95 • 254 PP. • SOFTCOVER • 978-1-891824-23-4

Print Books: Visit Our Online Bookstore www.LightTechnology.com
eBooks Available on Amazon, Apple iTunes, Google Play, and Barnes & Noble

$16.95
Plus Shipping
ISBN 13: 978-1-62233-017-1
Softcover 256 PP.
6 X 9 Perfect Bound

The Comprehension of the Holy Spirit within the Human Condition

Spirit of Space with Gabriel et al. through Arthur Fanning

TOPICS INCLUDE:

- The force of the Holy Spirit is coming: Are you ready?
- The forty-nine personalities in your chakras are unifying.
- Your soul force is expanding.
- Your birth name and birth date are vitally important.
- Your bones are becoming more fluid.
- The Moon rules the water in your body.
- Gratitude, appreciation, and prayer are essential now.
- Your thoughts: Are they yours or someone else's?
- All religions have the same god, the same idea, why fight?

And much, much more.

COMING SOON

Permission to Ascend

Spirit of Space with Gabriel et al. through Arthur Fanning

Phone: 928-526-1345 or 1-800-450-0985 • Fax: 928-714-1132

Light Technology PUBLISHING

12 Steps to a Lightness of Being

by Sarah Goddard Neves

This unique book has is a very special spiritual development course you take in the comfort of your own home. Through its wisdom and guided meditations — **included on the enclosed CDs to boost empowerment** — *12 Steps to a Lightness of Being* will gradually but surely lift your vibration and awaken you. To get the most out of this book, don't rush through it, but read it slowly. Take as long as you need each step before moving to the next. Commit to doing each meditation or visualization, giving yourself some quiet, undisturbed time to do this, and recall your meditation experiences and insights afterward. By doing so, you will get the most out of *12 Steps tp a Lightness of Being*.

$19.95 Plus Shipping

ISBN 13: 978-1-891824-99-9
Softcover • 160 pp.
6 X 9 Perfect Bound

The Twelve Steps:

1. Meditation on the Light
2. Opening to Your Intuition
3. Master Connection
4. Being Happy
5. The Healing Power of Forgiveness
6. Evolving with Love and Light
7. Realizing Your Life's Purpose
8. Awakening to Love
9. You: a Creation and a Creator
10. Soul Reflection
11. Hope from the Stars
12. Becoming a Lightness of Being

$25.00 Plus Shipping

ISBN 13: 978-1-891824-72-2
60 min. CD • 31 min. DVD
192 pp. • Spiral Bound

Includes CD & DVD

Handbook for Healers

by Frankie Z Avery & the OMA Group

Accompanied by an instructional DVD and a healing tones CD, the *Handbook for Healers* is intended for healers of all skill levels. OMA, channeled through Frankie Z Avery, offers advice on such issues as nutrition, lifestyle, and healing techniques. The companion DVD contains demonstrations of each of the meditations and exercises included. The *Healing Room Tones* CD is a creation of unique frequencies meant to enhance balance, harmony, and depth of perception in the healing room.

CHAPTERS INCLUDE:

- What Distinguishes Healers
- What Healers Do
- How Healing Works
- The Healer
- The Healer with a Patient
- Optimized Healing Environments
- Happiness
- The Importance of Eating Well

EXERCISES INCLUDE:

- Energize Your Day
- Check for Balance
- Expand Energy before Session
- Focus
- Balance with the Patient
- Stroke and Seal
- Cleanse between Patients
- Dust Off after Healing
- Restore: Catch Your Breath

Light Technology PUBLISHING Presents

Websites That Inform and Enrich

www.LightTechnology.com

- Discover the best channeled and inspired books of wisdom
- Find in-depth book information, including excerpts and contents

www.SedonaJournal.com

- Read advance excerpts of monthly channeling and predictions
- Order and access your electronic subscription

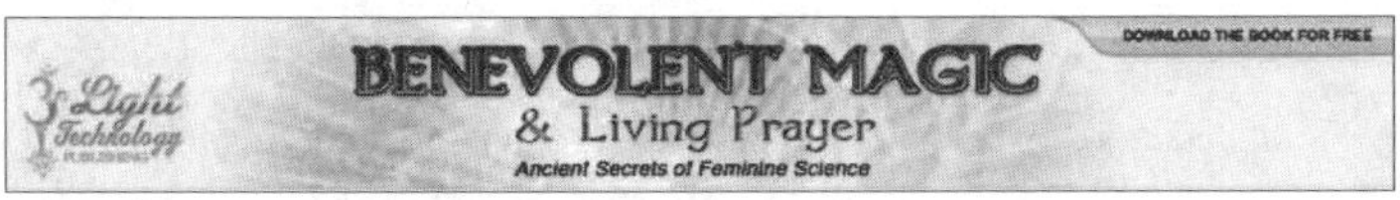

www.BenevolentMagic.com

- Learn the techniques of benevolence toward self and others that will help you create global peace
- Download the techniques of benevolent magic and living prayer for FREE!

www.ExplorerRace.com

- Discover your purpose, history, and future through the Explorer Race series
- Download the first chapter of each book for FREE!

www.ShamanicSecrets.com

- Learn about your natural self, and identify your natural talents and abilities
- Download the first chapter of each book for FREE!

Print Books: Visit Our Online Bookstore www.LightTechnology.com
eBooks Available on Amazon, Apple iTunes, Google Play, and Barnes & Noble